Praise for *Own Your Armor*

MW01233343

A master class on team dynamics in a picture book—yes! Only someone with Michelle Brody's experience and wisdom could do that! Read this book and learn from the best!

Amy Hayes, Global Head of Learning and
Development at Meta (Facebook)

Working closely and intensively with Michelle early in my senior management career was a formative experience. Not only did she have an intuitive understanding of what makes people and teams work, but she also made the process fun and entertaining. Her illustrated book follows this same pattern—it's fun, insightful, pragmatic and, in the end, enchantingly helpful.

Roy Harvey, CEO Alcoa

This ground-breaking book is an incredible contribution to our field. *Own Your Armor* reveals with great clarity and precision the fundamental drivers of dysfunctional behaviors on teams, the common interpersonal conflicts in the work-place, and the pervasiveness of fear in corporate life. Wise and compassionate, it offers an accessible understanding of psychological defenses, how they are evoked by modern day workplaces and can lead to toxicity on teams. *Own Your Armor* will swiftly take its rightful place as a seminal book on organizational culture and will enable executive teams to address, at their root, the inhibitors to trust, authenticity and high performance.

Amy Elizabeth Fox, CEO, Mobius Executive Leadership

A wonderful book, so full of insight and humanity. *Own Your Armor* is a delightful and informative look at the psychological dynamics of work teams. The lucid writing and engaging illustrations will leave you educated, entertained and with new tools to make an immediate difference in your functioning as a leader or team member--and in the other relationships in your life."

William J. Doherty, Ph.D., Professor, University of
Minnesota, Director of the Minnesota Couples on the
Brink Project, and Co-Founder of Braver Angels

I had never realized the immense impact of the 'armor' I bring to both my personal and professional life, before reading this book. Michelle Brody brings decades of hands-on research into this incredibly easy-to-read and practical guide that should be read and re-read by every leader. If you are a leader, buy *Own Your Armor*, and you'll better understand the unique challenges and motivations of your team—and how to grow as a leader.

David Siegel, CEO of Meetup, Author of *Decide and Conquer*

With *Own Your Armor*, Michelle Brody has done a great service for every team on the planet. This book identifies specific suits of armor people commonly don in response to the threats they perceive. People can easily see themselves, their armor, why they wear it, and most importantly, how they can get out of it. This wonderfully insightful and illustrated book should become a standard team operating manual.

Charles Feltman, Executive and Team Coach,
author of *The Thin Book of Trust*

What a brilliant and creative idea to take what we as psychologists know about successfully helping families and apply it to helping workplace teams. You and your team are sure to benefit from understanding and utilizing the lessons of "Owning Your Armor".

Dr. Dorothy Cantor, Former President of the
American Psychological Association

I've never been more hopeful at the possibilities of creating a dream team in my company. Dr. Brody has an innate ability to untangle the complexities of human dynamics and provide a clear path towards a much improved work environment. Brilliant in its approach, thank you Dr. Brody!

Ted Miller, CEO of Datakey Consulting, a growth accelerator firm

OWN YOUR
ARMOR

OWN YOUR
ARMOR

REVOLUTIONARY CHANGE FOR
WORKPLACE CULTURE

MICHELLE BRODY, PhD

Own Your Armor: Revolutionary Change for Workplace Culture

Published by LightChannel Press

Printed in the United States of America.
First paperback edition June 2022.

Illustrations by Lisa Naffziger.

Cover and layout design by G Sharp Design, LLC.
www.gsharpmajor.com

ISBN: 978-0-578-28886-4 (paperback)
ISBN: 979-8-218-00172-8 (hardcover)

Library of Congress Control Number: 2022906869

To Hal
and
to Eva, Jesse and Lev

Does this look familiar?

Here's a team with a culture gone bad.

The air is full of judgment, grievances, alliances, unproductive competition, and stalled decision-making.

And communication? No one says what they really mean, except when they are gossiping in the coffee room or in backchannels.

There's unprofessional behavior and finger pointing: *He won't take feedback. She's holding information to herself. He's too political. She is too slow.*

Everyone senses the missing trust, and it seriously affects the team's productivity. Work gets held up, and all that walking on eggshells means any one person can't get their job done without navigating other people's personalities. It's exhausting.

If you are a member of a team like this...

...you assume the leader has to solve it—that's their job! You are probably annoyed that they haven't fixed it already.

If you are the leader of a team like this...

...you likely have tried a few things already—and have been aggravated that the culture remains unchanged. You've given it time, you've disciplined some troublemakers, you've asked everyone to improve their communication and collaboration, you've even let some people go, but nothing seems to work. In desperation, you call for an offsite retreat. You wonder if that might shake things up—getting everyone out of the office, connecting as people, and talking about the culture problem directly.

Retreats for team culture often look like this.

The leader sets the agenda and everyone participates in collaborative work on the building blocks that should change the culture:

- **"Let's set clearer goals that everyone can align to."**
- **"Let's make a better communication strategy."**
- **"We've got to organize our processes so things run more smoothly."**
- **"Let's find ways to encourage better exchange of ideas."**
- **"We need more accountability if we are every going to be fully productive."**
- **"We have to stamp out bad behavior with better systems for feedback."**

The team gets to work. Everyone contributes to the discussion, and great ideas and plans emerge. The offsite ends with some clear commitments and solid buy-in. Everyone celebrates a great meeting with drinks and goes home feeling more connected and hopeful.

Monday comes.

You come back from the offsite and work to implement all those great ideas. At first, some things improve, but strangely, the culture problems still don't budge. Policies that should help communication don't change how people communicate. The smoother meetings you planned on the offsite don't actually happen. People drift from adhering to the new process plan. After a few weeks, the agreements you made to keep everyone accountable start slipping.

The leader is frustrated and a sense of hopelessness descends on the team. The bad culture seems stronger than anything you try to do to extinguish it. Now people start pointing fingers at what is making things so stuck:

- **"There are some really difficult personalities here."**
- **"It's the leader's weak leadership."**
- **"There is real change-aversion in this team."**

There may indeed be change aversion, imperfect leaders, and tough personalities, but that framing of the problem makes it only more unsolvable, and the culture more treacherous. Everyone suspects the inevitable: heads will roll. But whose? Cue more finger pointing, self-protection, manipulation, and undermining behavior...

Why does the Monday-after-the-offsite phenomenon happen? Because the approach isn't getting to the root of the problem.

As an executive coach and psychologist, I get called in to help teams when the people dynamics have gotten so disruptive that they can't be ignored. I help teams find the true causes of the bad culture and help them move toward greater health.

There are a lot of books for leaders on "how to fix your team" when "they" are difficult, which suggests that *the team is the problem* and *the leader is the change agent*, pushing or pulling *strategic levers* to improve the situation.

This book takes a dramatically different approach to solving team dynamics problems:

- the problem isn't just the team,
- the solution isn't just the leader's,
- and the levers aren't "strategic."

In the Own Your Armor approach:

- **Both leaders and team members contribute to the problem, and both are the change agents.** By definition, people dynamics are *dynamic*—they are co-created by those involved and are circularly reinforcing over time. Unwinding them requires everyone—leaders and team members—to recognize their contribution to the culture problem and to rejoin the team with their best self.

- **The levers that unlock team dynamics aren't strategic, but psychological.** As a psychologist who has worked with global teams, complicated couple conflicts, and polarized communities, I have seen what unlocks stuck dynamics. The Own 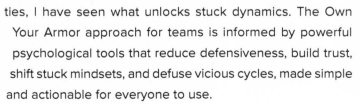 Your Armor approach for teams is informed by powerful psychological tools that reduce defensiveness, build trust, shift stuck mindsets, and defuse vicious cycles, made simple and actionable for everyone to use.

The root of team dynamics problems is almost always a pileup of ARMOR.

The rest of this book will explain how, but here is a quick overview:

- We all can show up as our regular selves at work, but when we are under threat, we put on some armor.

- We all armor up in different ways, but armored behavior comes across as less professional behavior than how any of us would be in our natural selves.

- Armored behavior from anyone on a team sets off a chain reaction, impacting others, and causing more armoring, until the whole team is locked up in cycles of defensive, tense interaction.

- For a team to take off armor to restore good communication, armor has to be OWNED. Owning armor means understanding what caused you to put it on and being able to speak about the impact it has on others.

- A team leader's armor has tremendous impact on a team's culture, so it also needs to change to fix the team's dynamic.

- Owning armor changes team culture, unlocks everyone's true potential, and restores optimal team productivity.

TABLE OF CONTENTS

THE OWN YOUR ARMOR PRINCIPLES

PRINCIPLE #1: TABLE

**Under-the-Table Dynamics Can't Be Solved
with Above-the-Table Strategies** *p. 18*

PRINCIPLE #2: THREATS

**Threats and Armor
Drive Bad Team Dynamics** *p. 26*

PRINCIPLE #3: ARMOR

**"Bad Apples" Are Usually Just Good
People Trying to Protect Themselves** *p. 38*

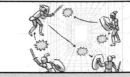

PRINCIPLE #4: EVERYONE

**Everyone On the Team
Contributes to the Dynamics** *p. 70*

PRINCIPLE #5: CYCLE

**Armor is Both a Response to Threat and
a Cause of Threat, Causing Cycles** *p. 98*

PRINCIPLE #6: INDIVIDUAL OWNING

**To Change Dynamics, Armor Needs
to Be Individually Owned** *p. 108*

PRINCIPLE #7: THREE PARTS OF OWNING

**Own Your Threats, Own Your Armor,
Own Your Impact** *p. 114*

PRINCIPLE #8: COMMUNICATION

**"Good Communication"
Is Unarmored** *p. 150*

PRINCIPLE #9: LEADER ARMOR

**Leader Armor has an Outsized
Impact on the Team** *p. 178*

PRINCIPLE #10: TEAM STRENGTH

**Owning Armor Unlocks
Team Strengths** *p. 186*

OWN YOUR
ARMOR

PRINCIPLE #1

TABLE

**Under-The-Table Dynamics
Can't Be Solved With
Above-The-Table Strategies**

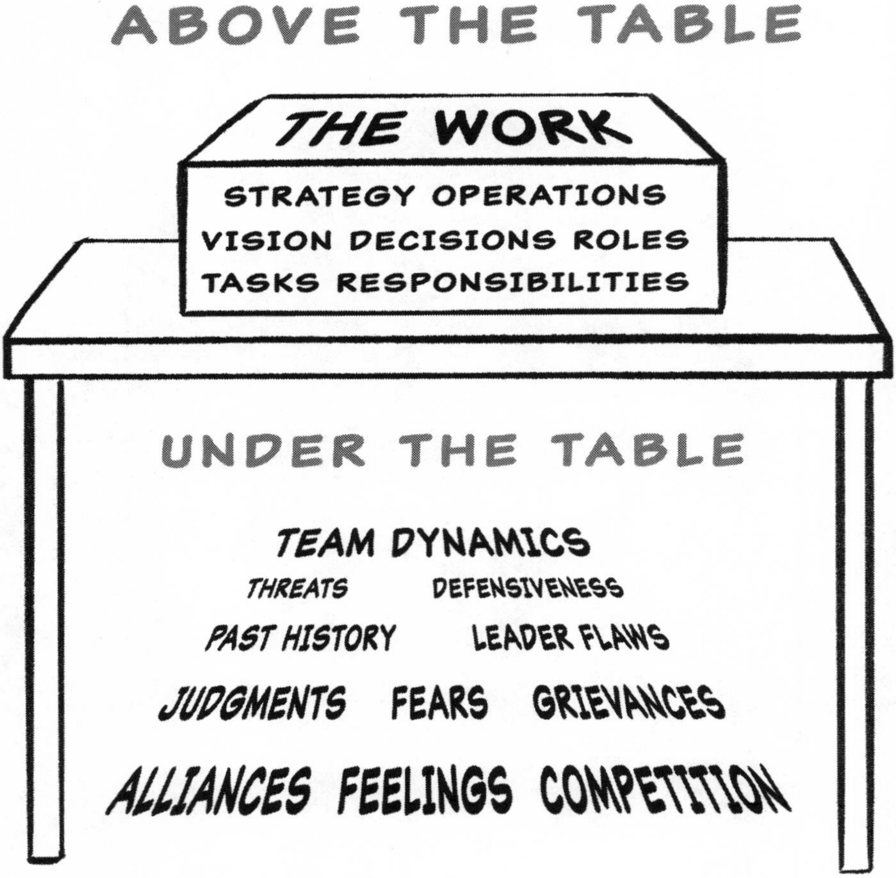

ABOVE THE TABLE

THE WORK

STRATEGY OPERATIONS
VISION DECISIONS ROLES
TASKS RESPONSIBILITIES

UNDER THE TABLE

TEAM DYNAMICS

THREATS   DEFENSIVENESS

PAST HISTORY   LEADER FLAWS

JUDGMENTS   FEARS   GRIEVANCES

ALLIANCES FEELINGS COMPETITION

Focusing on what's above the table isn't going to solve what's under the table.

Above the Table are all the communications spoken out loud about the work we are doing, the strategy we are creating or implementing, the decisions we are debating, the business we are executing. It's "professional work," and it's why we are all here.

And then there's everything going on Under the Table: the opinions, the alliances, the rivalries, the aggravation about past events, the fear about the future, the judgments, the assumptions about what the leader thinks about each person, what each member thinks about the leader (and each other), the social dynamics, the feelings, the threats, the interpersonal nets, the stuck patterns of interaction.

Although what's Under the Table is typically left unsaid, it's still "communicated" in that it seeps into the work. Nico darts a knowing look at Mara when Clyde presents ideas. Pat interrupts Kim to correct her. Gayle keeps her laptop open and texts Saul some strong opinions when the leader reviews the agenda. All signs of Under-the-Table action.

Under-the-Table is a land we don't like to visit.

It's messy down there, it feels seriously off topic, and it's a dumpster fire of emotions and grievances. We much prefer the Above-the-Table discussion, where we get to be our professional selves and use tools from our professional toolbox, like new policies or procedures.

But those interventions tend not to touch the fire. All those agreements sketched out on whiteboards at retreats? They're all usually Above-the-Table stuff. And the fire continues to rage.

If you really want to change your culture
and your team dynamics...

...you're going to have to make a trip Under-the-Table.

When you get there, you'll see that the fire is actually the chaos of every-one's armor clashing as they protect themselves from threats.

How can we understand what is happening Under the Table? The key is to focus on just two simple questions:

- **What threats are people responding to?**
- **What kind of armor are people putting on in response to those threats?**

Threats and armor are the twin engines of all Under-the-Table drama. Understand those, and you can begin to extinguish the fire.

OWN YOUR
ARMOR

PRINCIPLE #2

THREATS

**Threats and Armor Drive
Bad Team Dynamics**

Threats at Work

Work is an arena where we can earn a livelihood and experience some sense of stability, status, dignity, or success. It can also be a social environment where we can feel valued or experience belonging.

With so much at stake, work holds a lot of potential threats: losing your job; failure; or being thwarted, humiliated, excluded, undervalued, or unjustly treated. It's human instinct to self-protect against even the possibility of any of these threats.

THREATS AT WORK

LIVELIHOOD
oss of job or pay

SUCCESS
Thwarted or limited achievement

STABILITY
Chaos, disorganization, unclear expectations

CONTROL
Overpowered, nable to manage your own fate

DIGNITY
Loss of status, humiliation

REPUTATION
Misjudged, blamed for mistakes, seen as less successful than you know you can be

AUTONOMY
Controlled by others

FAIRNESS
Unfair treatment, unfair loss to others

HARMONY
Conflict, interpersonal tension

BELONGING
Excluded, not seen as a part of the team

AUTHORITY
Not respected by subordinates

How We Armor Up

At the Core, most people are reasonable, friendly, hardworking, and have every intention of doing a good job at work. But when we experience a threat, we go into an armored state to protect ourselves from that threat. We do whatever we can to manage the fear and preserve our ability to survive, keep our social connections, and succeed.

The armor we choose tends to be aligned with our preferences for fight or flight in stressful situations. Some people prefer to "fight," or move toward the situation, by actively defending their turf, strongly advocating for their point of view, or taking forward action to tackle problems. Some people prefer "flight," or to move away from the situation, by avoiding conflictual relationships, tuning out pressure, separating themselves from drama, or just focusing on their own work. Threats can also cause us to "freeze," temporarily not responding at all, until we settle into either a fight or a flight reaction.

NO THREAT, NO ARMOR!

THREAT APPEARS...

...SO ARMOR DEVELOPS.

ARMORED AGAINST THE THREAT!

Threat to LIVELIHOOD

Your promotion keeps getting stalled, which causes major financial loss.

ARMOR [FLIGHT]

Reduce effort so you aren't "underpaid" for your work. Care less about outcomes if no one cares about you.

Threat to SUCCESS

Peers are working at half-capacity, and that leaves you with more of a load.

ARMOR [FIGHT]

Advocate strongly or compete to get more resources for yourself.

Threat to FAIRNESS

Peers are constantly advocating for resources, and you feel you have to be strategic to get your fair share.

ARMOR [FLIGHT]

Keep information to yourself so you can act on it before others can use it for their purposes.

How Threats Create Armor: Some Examples

These are some common automatic reactions to threats at work. As you can see, both fight and flight armored reactions are natural, intuitive, and logical ways good people use to get through the day when things are tough. But although these reactions are understandable, armored behavior tends to look a lot less "professional" than what any of us would do when operating from our Core self. Reducing effort, avoiding others, deflecting feedback, competing for resources, and intentionally keeping information to yourself is not anyone's best behavior. Armor is justified on the inside (to self-protect), but it almost always irritates others on the outside.

Threat to AUTONOMY/ DIGNITY

Your manager is controlling and micromanaging, as if you don't know how to do this job without guidance on your every move.

ARMOR [FLIGHT]

Avoid them, do what you know is right to do rather than follow orders.

Threat to AUTHORITY

Your team says "yes" in meetings and then does what they want, disrespecting your authority.

ARMOR [FIGHT]

More closely monitor and manage their workflow to be sure to keep them accountable to commitments.

Threat to BELONGING

You aren't invited to key meetings, and it seems like you are being intentionally excluded.

ARMOR [FIGHT]

When you have the opportunity, talk up your accomplishments so that people know you have what it takes to be included.

Threat to REPUTATION

You just got a worse performance evaluation than you deserve.

ARMOR [FIGHT AND FLIGHT]

Deflect feedback, explain that peers withheld information that you need to succeed.

Your armored self is a little like your Evil Twin.

It's absolutely not the real you, but it looks like you on your worst day. You "become" your Evil Twin when you are irritated or under threat. When the threat goes away, you don't need the armor, and you can return to your Core, your real self. You know that your own Evil Twin behavior is in response to something tough around you.

But sometimes we mistake our coworker's armored Evil Twin for who they really are.

"He is so immature."
"She is explosive."
"He is always so critical."
"She can't get things done without a million questions."

The Evil Twin interpretation is so common that we forget the "Good Twin": the version of our colleagues who is a reasonable person responding to reasonable threats.

Dysfunctional Teams Are Armored

As a team coach and psychologist, my first assumption with dysfunctional teams is that everyone is acting with emotional logic: people are experiencing threat and are assuring their own protection with some kind of armor. The armor may not be pretty, but it's happening for an emotionally logical reason. "Bad behavior" is most often someone's armor; Evil Twins are reacting to something.

To disentangle the bad dynamics, my first task is to understand all the threats the team and its members are experiencing, whether these threats are from outside the team or generated between team members. If those threats can be defused, there will be less need for armor, and people's Core selves—their best selves—can return.

The dysfunction on the team comes from the armor, not from "bad people."

OWN YOUR
ARMOR

PRINCIPLE #3

ARMOR

**"Bad Apples" Are Usually
Just Good People Trying
to Protect Themselves**

The Bad Apple Fallacy

When a culture is dysfunctional, we naturally look around for the cause of the problem, and that often means looking for culprits. Whose behavior is causing pain to others? Who isn't working hard enough? Who is not a team player? Whose actions drive everyone else the most crazy?

Those are the "bad apples," and all the other team members are the "good apples"—the reliable, reasonable, and productive people. If you ask a team what needs to change to improve the culture, everyone has the "bad apples" in mind as they say things like "we need to work harder," "we need to cooperate more," or "we need to respect each other."

But what happens when you talk to the supposed "bad apples" on a team? I do this a fair amount as a team coach, and no surprise, I almost always learn there is a threat backstory and the "bad behavior" is some kind of armor.

If real change in team dynamics is what we are after, we are much better off looking for problematic interactions between armored *good* people than looking for "bad apples" or "unprofessional personalities."

To truly retire the "bad apple" fallacy, let's look at an example of a team where there's some troubling behavior.

THE TEAM

THE *GOOD*
WORKERS

THE PROBLEM
WORKERS

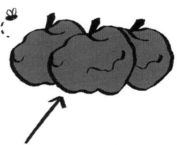

INTUITIVE PLAN: FIX THESE!

Meet the Members of an Armored Team

Here are eight colleagues who work together on a team with a lot of challenging dynamics. If you were to interview the team members, each one would tell you their complaints about the "bad behavior" of at least a few others. That bad behavior causes trouble (threat), so other team members respond to it with self protection (armor).

Everyone has a different type of armor on this team, but each type is a common type of work armor. As you meet this team, you will likely see some similarities with people at your workplace, or perhaps even with yourself.

You'll also notice that every one of these people is a good person handling common situations at work and trying to manage the challenges as best as they can.

Let's meet three of the so-called "bad apples": Sandhya, Grace, and Carl.

The Chaos Clearer

When Sandhya looks around her organization, she sees so many things that don't run as they should: processes are outdated, coworkers are slow, and mistakes slip by and cause costly inefficiencies. It makes every day agitating and frustratingly unproductive, especially since she is a person who cares about getting results. So she does what she feels she has to do: armor up and fight the battle against chaos.

The Armored Chaos Clearer: The Micromanager

Sandhya's armor is of the "fight" type: taking action against the threats to success around her. She tries to restore some reasonable order to a chaotic situation. She takes charge of improving processes, pushes for quicker problem-solving, gives feedback to others about mistakes or ways to improve, offers reminders of what needs to get done, and monitors progress to prevent chaos. These are all reasonable ways of dealing with a frustrating environment and the threat of failing to meet key outcomes. She might succeed in reducing the chaos and getting some things done.

But Sandhya's armor has strong impact on her teammates and might even drive them to be less productive. She comes across as controlling, commanding, and critical, and people around her feel judged, overridden, undervalued, micromanaged, and less motivated to join her.

The Thwarted Achiever

Like her colleague Sandhya, Grace is also driven by results and has always done well at work, but in this job she feels totally thwarted. It almost seems like the system is designed to work against her. Team members don't do their part. Cross-functional partners work at cross purposes and make success in her role really difficult.

She's boxed in, and it makes her performance look bad, which feels totally unfair. She's got to defend herself, so she armors up and speaks up—but in a different way than Sandhya.

The Armored Thwarted Achiever: The Finger Pointer

Grace points out that she could accomplish so much more if she wasn't so boxed in. She talks about the real problems that explain her less-than-ideal productivity: if there were more resources, or more cooperative partners, *then* she could get the job done properly. She registers legitimate complaints about how the system is impossible.

But to everyone around her, it just looks like she's making excuses, pointing fingers, and deflecting blame for her own performance. And all that finger pointing puts everyone else's reputations at risk too.

The Pressured New Guy

Carl is eager to show he was the right hire for this job.
He knows he has a lot to offer, but he hasn't had enough
opportunities to show his abilities. He's starting to get
some feedback that he isn't doing as well as he thinks.
His reputation is at risk, so he needs to show his value
to the company quickly. The pressure is on. He's frankly
a bit anxious, but no one is going to see that ...

The Armored Pressured New Guy: The Flexer

To protect himself, Carl armors up. He makes sure that the higher-ups know what he's working on, highlights his accomplishments in meetings, and advocates strongly for access to the resources he needs to succeed. He strategizes to be given the highest-priority work so he can show his value. If he gets feedback that he didn't do something well, he'll push back ("Can you give me even one example of that?") or point out what he did that was justified.

These are all reasonable ways to protect himself from the threat to his reputation.

But to the team, Carl is a flexer: boastful, self-promoting, land-grabbing, and not a team player. It's impossible to give him constructive feedback because he seems to push back on anything that implies that he has done something less than perfectly. His flexing armor tosses threats to others, who then say, "He's taking credit for my work," "He's moving into my lane," "If he's so 'perfect,' then his mistakes will be blamed on us!" or "You have to really compete against him, or you'll lose resources."

"Bad Behavior" as Self-Protective Armor

Most people would label "micromanaging," "finger pointing," or "flexing" as unprofessional behavior. From the outside, Sandhya, Grace, and Carl look like problematic "bad apples" on the team. They annoy other team members (the seemingly "good apples") and add to an uncomfortable culture. But from their own perspective, they are just coping with some pretty frustrating threats and trying to make the best of it so they can get back to work and do well. At the Core, they are well-intentioned, but under threat, they need to self-protect and armor up. And their armor is causing problems.

If there was an offsite to deal with this team's culture, you can imagine that when the group discusses "what we will all do differently," what they really mean is what Grace and Sandhya and Carl should do differently: "Those 'bad apples' just need to shape up and be more like us good apples!"

But wait. Some of those "good apples" are the same people who are thwarting Grace, moving too slowly for Sandhya, or adding pressure for Carl. Are they totally blameless in this? Let's meet one of them. Alvaro drives Sandhya crazy because he seems to move in slow motion. But he too has a backstory.

THE TEAM

THE GOOD
WORKERS

THE PROBLEM
WORKERS

INTUITIVE PLAN: FIX THESE!

Feedback Flooded

Alvaro's reputation is under threat. He has been getting a lot of "constructive" feedback lately from all sides and is feeling deeply undervalued. He knows he has talent, and he's had great success in the past, but constantly hearing about what he could be doing better is undermining his usual confidence. A little more positive feedback, encouragement, or faith in him would go a long way to getting him back on track. But no. Every slight mistake gets highlighted, nothing he does seems good enough, and the criticism stings. The constant pressure to fight the unfair reputation forming around him is demoralizing and trips him up more than he'd like to admit. So he armors up.

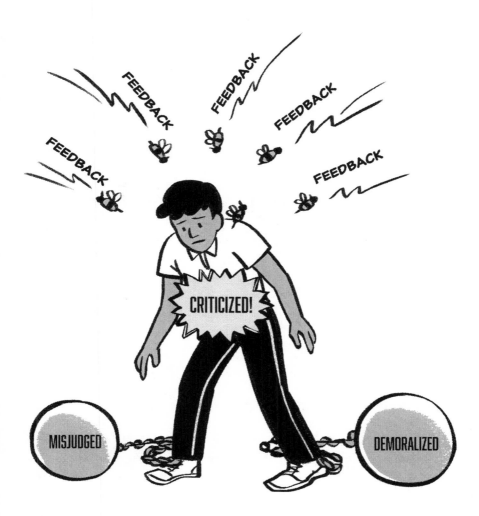

Armored Feedback Flooded: The Non-Initiator

Alvaro's armor is of a "flight" type: he moves away from the threat to his reputation by getting cautious. He takes it slower and triple checks his work so he can be sure he won't make a mistake. It's time consuming, but that strategy protects him from extra "stings" of critique. If people always think your idea is wrong, best to wait for guidance before starting anything and not to expend too much effort on the first draft of anything. All very reasonable steps to avoid the ongoing threat to his reputation.

But to everyone else, it looks like Alvaro never takes initiative, goes too slowly, and is lazy and unproductive. His teammates conclude he could use some *more* feedback about his performance, which is the last thing he wants.

Now imagine what happens when a Chaos Clearer like Sandhya works with someone who is Feedback Flooded like Alvaro. Pretty predictably, the armor they use to solve for the threats they feel gets them stuck in a cycle like this. You could call it the **Charging and Dodging Cycle**.

Sandhya charges forward, anxious about getting the project done, and already sees that the pace is behind schedule. She's especially frustrated by Alvaro, the slowest member of the team. No matter what she does to get him to move faster or be more productive, it never works. In fact, when she stays on top of reminding or directing him, he seems to go even slower!

On his side, Alvaro feels constantly stung with judgment, pressure, and control, and the more Sandhya hounds him, the more he feels demoralized and

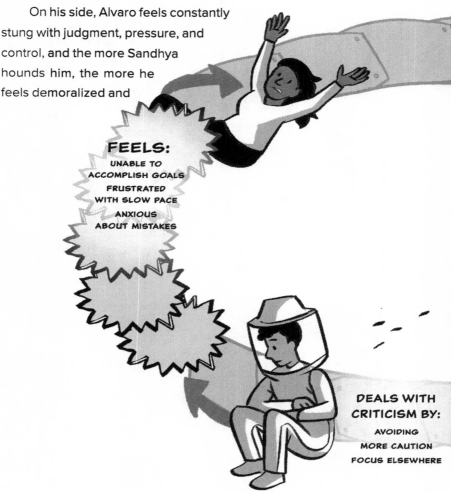

FEELS:
UNABLE TO
ACCOMPLISH GOALS
FRUSTRATED
WITH SLOW PACE
ANXIOUS
ABOUT MISTAKES

DEALS WITH
CRITICISM BY:
AVOIDING
MORE CAUTION
FOCUS ELSEWHERE

exhausted. Feeling it will be a long (and impossible) road to succeeding in Sandhya's eyes, he starts dodging interactions with her, avoiding her as much as possible, slowing a bit to push back on her urgency. To avoid mistakes and her criticism, he gets extra cautious in his work with her and tries to focus his energy elsewhere. That feeds right into her fears that he will be no help on the looming disaster of this project, and she responds with more feedback and pressure for speed, which demoralizes Alvaro more.

A cycle like this can get pretty stuck, with neither of them really able to change it. Both are trying to solve for the problem they experience, but their solutions work against each other, inadvertently co-creating a vicious armored cycle.

REGAIN CONTROL BY:
MONITORING
REMINDING
CORRECTING
DIRECTING

FEELS:
PRESSURED
JUDGED
DEMORALIZED
EXHAUSTED
CONTROLLED

The longer cycles like this go on, the more the relationship devolves into pervasive and generalized mistrust.

The armor gets thicker, the shields get bigger, and the swords get more menacing. As a result, each person looks more and more threatening to the other, so there is even more need to keep the armor on.

Now, it's not just what they *do* that aggravates the other. Eventually, they write each other off as people:

"I can't respect or trust you at all."

"We obviously don't share any values."

"There is something seriously wrong with you."

When the mistrust gets to this level, armor can show up as even more problematic behavior, like open backstabbing, attempts to discredit each other in public or with other stakeholders, or a refusal to work together.

So which one is the "bad apple"?

The answer is neither. Sandhya micromanages because Alvaro is slow moving. Alvaro is slow moving because Sandhya is micromanaging. They are both *good people* at the Core, showing up in their armor for good reason because of the threats they feel.

Neither one is to blame for creating the situation, but neither is blameless. They are both inadvertently co-creating a vicious cycle. Or more precisely, their threats and armor are the twin engines that are co-creating the vicious cycle.

So what can be done to stop a cycle like this? The key to unlocking the stuck cycle is for each person to **own their threats**, **own their armor**, and **own their impact**. How to do so is coming up in Principle 7.

But first, there is even more complexity on this team than just this one two-person cycle. There are four other team members that bring their own contributions to the team dynamics and those vicious cycles.

OWN YOUR
ARMOR

PRINCIPLE #4

EVERYONE

Everyone on the Team
Contributes to the Dynamics*

*Even "perfectly professional,"
"righteous," or quiet people.

When I talk about the Everyone Contributes principle with a team, someone will always raise this question.

"Sure," they'll say, "Carl is a jerk and Sandhya is controlling, Grace makes excuses and Alvaro is slow, but I'm just a regular person who isn't doing anything wrong." Usually that is followed by something like:

> **"In fact, I'm a person who is just doing my job and not getting involved in the dynamics."**
>
> or
>
> **"I'm actually a person who is actively trying to make things better around here!"**

Unfortunately, even these strategies for dealing with team tension also impact others and contribute to the culture. There are a few people of these types on our example team. Let's meet them.

The Deep Focuser

Kaila wishes she could do her work in peace. Her best work comes when she can deeply focus and dig into the detail of what she is doing. Her micromanaging, finger pointing, and boasting coworkers (like Sandhya, Grace, and Carl) add so much thrash to the environment that it's impossible to concentrate. Even when working from home, there are constant intrusions—endless reminder pings, requests for nonsense work, unnecessary meetings and urgency to have whatever they need RIGHT NOW! So Kaila does what any logical person would. She armors up and tunes them out.

The Armored Deep Focuser: The Lone Wolf

Kaila focuses on her own work and manages her time so she can be optimally productive. She answers emails only twice a day and avoids communicating with people who will take up her time or prevent her from doing her job well. She doesn't respond reflexively to other people's "urgent" requests that seem pointless—that would just encourage them to keep firing more. If she shares progress on her work, it tends to get endlessly commented about by the others and she ends up having to do it again, so she has learned to submit things closer to the due date to avoid rework.

It's an efficient and reasonable way of dealing with a frustrating environment and the constant threat of intrusion.

But her teammates are aggravated by her armor. She's seen as a lone wolf, uncommunicative, not a team player. She creates duplication of work because she never shares her work in time for others to use it productively, and you can't really count on her to be flexible to help others succeed.

The Principled Warrior

Justine feels strongly that things aren't very fair at her workplace, and frustratingly, management doesn't do anything about it. That's why the culture is so bad here, in her opinion. No one is making sure that everyone follows office protocols, or that projects get assigned with equity, or that promotion criteria are clear. Justine herself feels overburdened with extra work as a result, and she suspects she isn't compensated as well as some of her peers. No one else seems to have the energy or courage to do something about it, so Justine armors up to make things better for all with a principled fight.

The Armored Principled Warrior: The Complainer

Justine's armor is of the "fight" type. She stands up for herself and others by speaking up and pushing for change. She asks questions, points out problems, and advocates strongly for what needs to happen to fix them. In meetings, she sometimes has to confront the leader, just to get some reasonable action. She particularly speaks up for team members (and herself) who aren't getting a fair shot at promotion. She tries to get others to join her...

...but the rest of the team tends to back away from joining her fight. She seems a little too aggressive and self-righteous in how she operates, and she complains a lot. Some find her tendency to call out leadership arrogant and inappropriate. Her constant advocating is exhausting, so they tend to stop listening. Management sometimes tries to appease her on various crusades, but mostly keeps their distance to avoid a fight, which only frustrates Justine more as she feels unheard and makes no progress on what matters most to her.

The Comforter

Alain has worked at places where he felt like part of a family; everyone looked out for everyone else. But here, it's toxic. No one seems to get along. The air is filled with conflict and tension, and there is no team cohesion to speak of. Many people have gripes, feel isolated, and are annoyed by colleagues who are competitive or self-interested. His deep belief: the team could do so much more if only we worked together! Alain himself is agitated by the lack of harmony in the team, so he armors up to try to help with the problem.

DISCORD!

The Armored Comforter: The Pot Stirrer

Alain actively tries to create community within the team by building alliances and engaging people socially to boost connections. He takes the time to hear everyone's complaints and calm people down so they feel heard, supported, and not alone. You want to complain about the leader? Alain is there for you. Moan about Carl's boasting? Sandhya's micromanaging? Grace's finger pointing? Kaila's disconnection? Justine's pushiness? Alvaro's laziness? Alain is in the coffee room, ready to serve as the sounding board for your irritations. It's an understandable response to deal with the pain of disharmony at work...

...but it also has the effect of stirring the pot. His colleagues (and leader) wonder if they are next to be gossiped about behind closed doors. While the team appreciates what a good guy Alain is, they also think he wastes time with all his counseling, doesn't pull his weight when there is work to be done, and ends up creating more drama.

The Drama Deflector

Tor loves his job, but the politics ... UGH! Everyone around him seems overly preoccupied with office drama. It feels like junior high school: people dwell on who's annoyed with whom, who the boss is favoring, and the latest gossip. It's agitating, super distracting, and a complete waste of time. Instead of losing his patience, he armors up.

EMOTIONAL OVERLOAD!

OBJECTIVITY

NO EMOTION

DATA

The Armored Drama Deflector: The Robot

Tor protects his focus from all the overemotional noise by staying super professional and above the fray. He prides himself on always acting rationally. He often has to remind coworkers to do so as well, since they seem to let their emotions drive their decision-making. Sometimes he has to actively change the subject when they obsess about "personnel impact" or "employee satisfaction" to remind people that this is work, we are all adults, and the goal isn't making sure everyone is happy. He often answers questions in a purely data-focused way to try to model professionalism. Tor's approach is a reasonable way to handle the discomfort of too much emotion and drama.

But to his teammates, Tor is transactional and concrete, and he seems often to miss the point, which makes problem solving with him extra challenging. When he does what he thinks "makes sense," he doesn't pay attention to the impact those actions might have on the rest of the team. When they try to give him feedback about how they have been affected, he dismisses it as irrelevant since only the work-related outcomes matter. It's so hard to get through to him!

"Just Trying To Do My Job" and "Just Trying To Help"

Justine, Tor, Alain, and Kaila might say, "Okay, maybe I'm contributing a little, but I'm certainly not as bad as Sandhya, Alvaro, Carl, and Grace, so I don't have to change as much as they do!" This might make them feel better about themselves, but it doesn't help solve the team problem. Armor is armor, and all types of it contribute to the dynamic. **Just as there are no "bad apples" who are causing *all* the trouble on the team, there are also no "good apples" who aren't causing *any* trouble.** Everyone can be good in their Core selves but also contributing to team trouble with their armor.

The next page summarizes the different types of armor on this sample team.

As you read it, keep in mind that these eight types are not an exhaustive list of all types of possible armor. Threats hit us in combinations, and we tend to use combinations of coping strategies (i.e., armor) to deal with them. Any one situation may feel like it has three different kinds of threats in it, as is the case for several of the people in this sample team. Also, people experience threats and respond to threats in a variety of different ways, so different people may respond to the same set of threats with different kinds of armor. In addition, any one person may use the same kinds of armor in all environments, or use different armor depending on the particular threats present in each environment.

For this specific sample team, the chart summarizes what important value is under threat for each person, how they understandably cope (their type of armor), and how their armor inadvertently complicates things for others on the team.

Team: Types of Armor

KEY VALUES AT STAKE   PERCEIVED THREATS

SUCCESS, CONTROL

IT SEEMS LIKE...
- Goals are challenging; progress toward them is too slow.
- Processes aren't smooth; there's chaos in the system.
- Others' less optimal efforts put your success at risk.

Experienced as risk of failure and loss of control.

SUCCESS, REPUTATION

IT SEEMS LIKE . . .
- Goals are challenging; progress toward them is too slow.
- Others' less optimal efforts put your success at risk.
- Obstacles around you make you look less productive.

Experienced as a risk of failure, and risk of being misjudged.

REPUTATION, SUCCESS

IT SEEMS LIKE...
- Performance feedback hasn't been as positive as expected.
- You feel your capabilities have been misunderstood.
- There's pressure to perform and to appear successful quickly.

Experienced as risk of being misjudged as failing or not meeting expectations.

REPUTATION CONTROL SUCCESS

IT SEEMS LIKE...
- Performance feedback has been negative and you feel misunderstood.
- Pressure to quickly fix your reputation creates anxiety, which makes it harder to perform, yielding more criticism.

Experienced as hopelessly trapped by endless criticism.

AUTONOMY, STABILITY, SUCCESS

IT SEEMS LIKE...
- Your boss or peers are controlling, pressuring, or micromanaging, which feels destabilizing and intrusive.
- Engaging with them only slows you down, makes it harder to do your job, and leads to redoing work.

Experienced as interference with your ability to control your own success.

FAIRNESS, LIVELIHOOD, SUCCESS

IT SEEMS LIKE...
- Compensation and promotion processes are unfair.
- Protocols aren't followed, so work is distributed unequally, and some are more burdened than others. No one else speaks up about it.

Experienced as unfair and limiting to livelihood and success.

HARMONY, BELONGING, SUCCESS

IT SEEMS LIKE...
- Instead of team cohesion, there is complaining, tension, and conflict, and some people aren't acting professionally.
- Success seems impossible in such a negative environment.
- Leader doesn't seem to make the changes necessary to improve things.

Experienced as isolating, agitating, and interfering with productivity.

STABILITY, SUCCESS

IT SEEMS LIKE...
- There is complaining, conflict, and emotional drama in the team, and some people aren't acting professionally.
- Time is wasted, stability is threatened, and the work gets derailed by all the overemotional drama.

Experienced as distracting and undermining of productivity.

COPING ACTIONS (ARMOR)	UNINTENDED IMPACT
SO UNDERSTANDABLY, YOU... • Push for results and take charge to accomplish the task. • Create/change processes quickly. • Direct, manage, or work around "thwarters."	**BUT UNFORTUNATELY, YOUR ARMOR...** • Threatens others by coming across as controlling, critical, undervaluing of others, or micromanaging.
SO UNDERSTANDABLY, YOU... • Point out the problems you see so that they can be fixed. • Make it clear you are being misjudged by clarifying that your success is impeded by outside obstacles or other people, not your own abilities.	**BUT UNFORTUNATELY, YOUR ARMOR...** • Threatens others by coming across as blaming, complaining, or not taking responsibility.
SO UNDERSTANDABLY, YOU... • Highlight achievements in meetings so your success gets noticed. • Downplay mistakes and push back against unfair negative feedback. • Make sure you get high-value work so you can stand out.	**BUT UNFORTUNATELY, YOUR ARMOR...** • Threatens others by coming across as self-promoting, overly competitive, land-grabbing, rejecting of feedback, and not a team player.
SO UNDERSTANDABLY, YOU... • Try to take control of the situation by being extra cautious, taking it slowly to avoid making mistakes. • Prevent criticism by asking for or waiting for guidance before starting in a wrong direction.	**BUT UNFORTUNATELY, YOUR ARMOR...** • Threatens others by coming across as slow moving, unproductive, unresponsive to feedback, and not taking initiative to contribute.
SO UNDERSTANDABLY, YOU... • Preserve your autonomy by avoiding those who are intrusive or controlling. • Just do your job and focus on your own deliverables. • Don't automatically respond to people's "emergencies."	**BUT UNFORTUNATELY, YOUR ARMOR...** • Threatens others by coming across as self-oriented, uncommunicative, and not willing to help others deliver what they need to deliver.
SO UNDERSTANDABLY, YOU... • Advocate strongly for more pay, promotion, or resources. • Find allies to speak out against injustice. • If leaders aren't responsive, take it to their superiors. • Highlight the obvious values that are being ignored.	**BUT UNFORTUNATELY, YOUR ARMOR...** • Threatens others by coming across as combative, self-righteous, complaining, or challenging to leaders.
SO UNDERSTANDABLY, YOU... • Try to create community by engaging with people • Become a good listener, letting people vent their complaints about the leader or about each other. • Help everyone feel heard and supported.	**BUT UNFORTUNATELY, YOUR ARMOR...** • Threatens others by coming across as stirring the pot and encouraging a culture of gossip and complaining. • Can be seen as wasting time on drama, undermining leaders, and not focusing enough on getting work done.
SO UNDERSTANDABLY, YOU... • Tune out the emotional noise by staying professional and objective. • Remind coworkers to focus on work, not pandering to people's "feelings." • Defend your solutions as the rational ones.	**BUT UNFORTUNATELY, YOUR ARMOR...** • Threatens others by coming across as indifferent to others' concerns/feelings, unwilling to listen, and dismissive of feedback that doesn't fit your definition of "rational."

You've now met the entire team: eight people trying to work together but struggling with one another. In reading about them, some of you might be thinking, "Whoa. There aren't just a few bad apples—they are *all* bad apples!" If you worked with this team, you might give up hope or wish they would just all leave the company, because as they say, "you can't change people's personalities."

Personality is indeed very hard to change. And if you had to change personalities to change team dynamics, you'd need a team of psychologists toiling in every office and no other work would get done. Fortunately, there is hope, because "bad personalities" aren't what's causing bad behavior on teams. It's good people with nice personalities getting armored.

Armoring is a state, not a personality trait. This is the fundamental mindset shift needed to help people change non-optimal behavior.

We can think of "bad behavior" as coming from a person's **traits** ("He's acting that way because he has bad character"), or as triggered by a person's **state** ("He's armored for some reason of threat or stress right now"). A "trait" approach to another person's non-optimal behavior tends to bring more defensiveness. A "state" approach tends to yield more responsibility-taking and change.

Here's an example. Imagine you are a leader, and a person on your team shows some kind of problematic behavior. Let's look at the two different mindsets about that "bad behavior".

The Key Mindset Shift: Bad Apple Or Armored?

"He is behaving badly because he is a bad worker, has a bad personality, or is missing essential people skills."

OPTIONS FOR FIXES

- Give feedback
- Get coaching for him to change his behavior
- Monitor or constrain his behavior
- Offer consequences for not changing
- If nothing improves, change his role or let him go

RISKS

- He resists feedback and armors more
- He can't stop the behavior because he needs it for self-protection, and armors more
- Behavior issues continue or escalate
- Mistrust grows in the leader-employee relationship

"He is behaving badly because he is armored. Something must be threatening him."

OPTIONS FOR FIXES

- Listen to him to understand the threats causing him to armor up
- Validate need for armor but point out unfortunate impact
- Share your belief that his Core self is much more effective than his armored state
- Help him to own his armor and its impact
- Help reduce threats that result in armor, so he can return to his more professional, unarmored self.

OPPORTUNITIES

- He feels understood
- He is motivated to return to unarmored self because his essential personality isn't being criticized
- He owns his armor and his impact
- Trust grows in the leader-employee relationship

When the leader approaches the employee with a mindset of "you are doing something wrong because you either don't know how to behave, are immature or don't have skill", the employee is more likely to defend why his behavior wasn't wrong, fighting the larger impli- cation that being wrong in this instance means they are truly unknowing, immature or unskilled. "It was justified" or "it was the only option" are logical self-defensive comments. The dialogue becomes about whether it was or was not reasonable to respond to the threat that way, and not about the impact the behavior had. When a leader approaches with, "How do we help you get back to your real self?" or "This was out of character for you, something must be going on", the employee will be much more likely to engage in discussing it. Taking responsibility becomes easier when we are owning our armor rather than owning being fundamentally wrong. The employee can more easily admit that unfortunately they got triggered, their worst side came out and it had negative impact on others.

OWN YOUR
ARMOR

PRINCIPLE #5

CYCLE

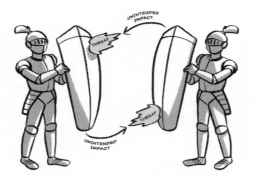

Team Dynamics Often
Involve Vicious Cycles...

**...because armor is both a response
to threat and a cause of more threat.**

Charging-Dodging Cycle

Remember the vicious cycle between Sandhya and Alvaro? As each person armored up to deal with their frustration, their armored behavior added threat for the other.

FEELS:
UNABLE TO ACCOMPLISH GOALS
FRUSTRATED WITH SLOW PACE
ANXIOUS ABOUT MISTAKES

DEALS WITH CRITICISM BY:
AVOIDING
MORE CAUTION
FOCUS ELSEWHERE

Threat/Armor cycles are a very common feature of all kinds of conflict (including between couples!)

When you feel threatened by the other person, you armor up, and the way you armor will annoy (and threaten) the other person so they armor up too. No one ever intends to create these vicious cycles but we get drawn into them easily because the need to protect against threat is very automatic.

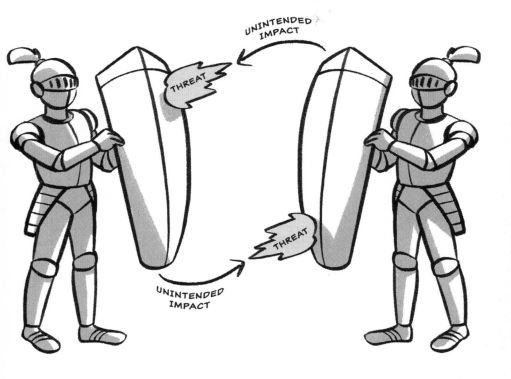

Team down a vortex:
Everyone's armor adds threat

Any vicious cycle between two people at work doesn't just affect those two individuals. It spreads to the team. For example, the more one person responds to threat by disengaging and sticking to their own job, the harder it is for the rest of the team to meet their objectives. The stress of possibly not meeting goals might cause someone else to more strongly direct others. Those who feel overly directed might complain to colleagues that the leader isn't managing the team well. The leader, feeling threatened, might make some role changes that anger others, and on and on. Everyone is naturally trying to improve things with their actions, but every armored action has the potential to generate more threats.

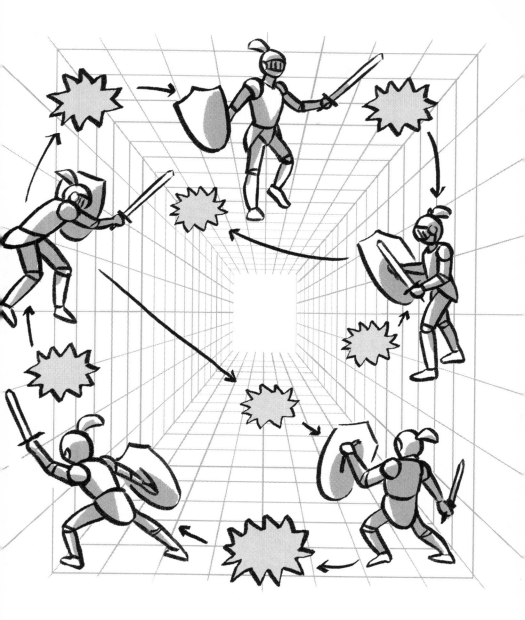

This, then, is the frustrating paradox of team culture problems: we react to bad culture with self-protection, and each individual's self-protection feeds more bad culture into the team. As mistrust grows, everyone has to armor up more, but then everyone looks less trustworthy to others, adding more threat! No one can take off their armor in such a threatening environment, but keeping it on makes matters worse for everyone on the team.

The only way out is **mutual disarmament**. Each person must take responsibility for their own armor and how it impacts the team.

OWN YOUR
ARMOR

PRINCIPLE #6

INDIVIDUAL OWNING

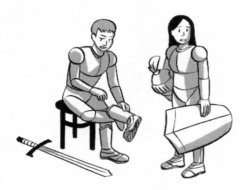

To Change Dynamics, Armor
Needs to be *Individually* Owned

*Leaders too. See Principle 9.

Remember the typical team offsite?

When the team makes an effort to work together to address the dynamics problems, it naturally leads to solutions like creating team commitments everyone should follow.

Imagine the kind of commitments that might come out in the brainstorming for the example team.

- "We need clearer lanes and more collaboration."
- "We all need to communicate more and better with each other."
- "People need to be more accountable."
- "Let's agree to truly be more respectful: no criticism, no gossip, no complaining."
- "Let's make sure things are fair."

Think now about how those team agreements would impact the individual armor causing trouble in this team. The team hopes Carl will especially take to heart the agreement about clearer lanes and more collaboration. Everyone hopes Alain will realize the gossip rule is mostly for him. Justine hopes everyone will join her in the fight for fairness.

But with commitments set as team guidelines, does Alvaro truly get that his behavior frustrates others? Do Tor and Grace realize everyone needs them to be more communicative? Does Justine understand that her justice-fighting adds an aggressive vibe to the team? Without individualizing accountability for each person's own armor and their specific impacts, none of these commitments are likely to yield change.

Your Role in the Whole

Team dynamics won't be solved by reminding people of the team norms or resetting them with collective, guideline-like language such as "we should all communicate more," or "we should follow processes," or "we should be more accountable." Instead, each person has to understand the role of their particular armor in the team dynamics and then take responsibility for changing that specific problematic contribution to the team culture.

You might think that the way to get each person to own their armor would be to give them individual feedback about it, something like: "Your armor is creating pressure for others," or "Your armor is slowing us down." But that feedback approach (either from leaders or peers) will not work and is more likely to backfire—causing more defensiveness than openness to change.

Owning your armor must begin as a *personal reflective process.* No one else needs to tell you that you sometimes don't operate at your best. You know what ticks you off, what annoying things at work push you into your armor and your not-best self. You might not consider how your armor affects others, because, like everyone, we focus on what is *justified* about our armored reactions ("I had to tune out the drama—how else could I work?!?") rather than how it might be creating threat for others in the team ("He just ignores what he doesn't want to attend to, and that's maddening!"). When you take the time to reflect on your own reactions, you can find the answer to the key armor-owning question:

How does my armor, my individual response to threat, intersect with everyone else's to co-create problematic dynamics on this team?

When every team member can answer that question, culture change becomes possible.

OWN YOUR
ARMOR

PRINCIPLE #7

THREE PARTS OF OWNING

**Own Your Threats,
Own Your Armor, and
Own Your Impact**

Your Armor

So let's talk about you.

Whether you're a leader or a member of a team, your team needs you to individually own your armor so that it stops impacting others. What does it mean to own your armor? It means:

- **Own your threats.**
- **Own your reactions to those threats (your armor).**
- **Own the way your armor impacts others.**

Own Your Armor Self-Assessment

As you read about the example team, you may have already started to recognize some threats and armor in yourself or others.

In this section, you'll have a chance to more thoroughly own your armor with a series of three self-assessments about the threats you experience, the armor you typically use, and the impact your armor may have. For each, look over the list and identify which items resonate for you. You might check them off or rewrite them to better describe your experience. On page 148, you'll find a worksheet for recording your reflections.

If you are using this book as prework for your team offsite, the observations you record about yourself will be the basis for some of the discussion with your team.

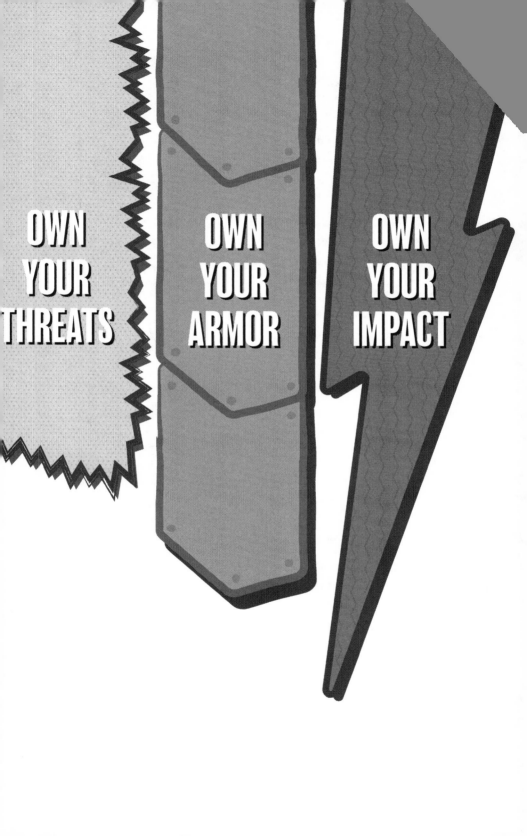

ır Threats

Let's start with what irks you.

Whether you are a leader or team member, you have to deal with certain pressures and stressors that can generate threats for you.

To identify your threats, here are some questions to consider:

- What are your greatest frustrations at work? Think back to the last time you were so frustrated at work you "lost it," or needed to vent about it at home. What happened that irked you?

- What do you want but aren't getting enough of (pay, path to success, recognition, status, autonomy, community, etc.)?

- Is there a particular person or persons you find especially annoying? Why? What do they do?

- What else might you consider a threat? Consider stressors that come from outside the team (market conditions, competitors), threats from within yourself (internal pressures), and threats that come about in relationships with coworkers.

Asking yourself "What irks me?" gets you to the first level of understanding the threats you most respond to. Notice that the natural expression of frustration is to point outward at the situations or people who are causing problems, with comments like "I can't stand people who slow down the work," "The worst leaders are the ones who try to embarrass people in meetings," or "Annual goal setting is just a way you can be blamed later for failure." But those situations "get" us and trigger a sense of threat because they link inward, to what is inside every one of us.

THREATS AT WORK

LIVELIHOOD
Loss of job or pay

SUCCESS
Thwarted or limited achievement

STABILITY
Chaos, disorganization, unclear expectations

CONTROL
Overpowered, unable to manage your own fate

DIGNITY
Loss of status, humiliation

REPUTATION
Misjudged, blamed for mistakes, seen as less successful than you know you can be

AUTONOMY
Controlled by others

FAIRNESS
Unfair treatment, unfair loss to others

HARMONY
Conflict, interpersonal tension

BELONGING
Excluded, not seen as a part of the team

AUTHORITY
Not respected by subordinates

The Depth of Threats: Longings and Sensitivities

Everyone has a set of life experiences that affect what they respond to today. Your life story—how you were raised, what your closest relationships were like, the challenges you faced, what you had and what you didn't have, the values you learned to hold dear, and all of your experiences in your family, at school, and at work—set you up for a unique set of longings and sensitivities.

"Whoa . . . who are you calling sensitive!? I'm not sensitive!" you might say. I don't mean sensitive in a needy sort of way. *Sensitivities* are the often-invisible personal feelings that make us susceptible to particular kinds of threats. Everyone has them. Similarly, *longings* are the deep desires that come from life experiences and drive what motivates us— what we strive for and what matters for us at work. Everyone has those too. Your unique set of longings and sensitivities sits inside your head until something happens at work that is particularly linked to them and boom, it feels more threatening than it might to those with a different set of longings and sensitivities.

As you consider what your threats are at work, it is helpful to reflect on why those situations or interactions are more likely to cause you to put on armor than others. There are likely some clues in your life story.

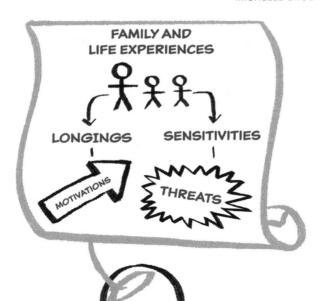

When you have had experience with...	These work situations can feel especially threatening...
Rigid rules of your culture limiting your opportunity *(sensitive to control, longing for autonomy)*	Thwarting by a rigid boss or rigid rules
Constant comparison to siblings *(sensitive to fairness, longing to stand out)*	Working with competitive peers or being compared to peers
Tragic mistake changing everything *(sensitive to chaos, longing for control)*	When others are disorganized or there is loose control over processes
A highly critical parent or previous boss *(sensitive to reputation, longing for praise)*	When criticized or debated while presenting work
Not being able to count on having money *(sensitive to loss of livelihood, longing for stability)*	Threats to compensation, or when others waste resources

OWN
YOUR
THREATS

Threats Self-Assessment Instructions

On the next page is a checklist of threatening experiences at work that can be triggers for putting on your armor. As you read through each situation, check those that are happening for you in some way on your work team. The list isn't exhaustive, so you'll likely think of ones that are particular to your situation.

After a first pass through the list, review what you have checked and highlight which situations are particularly frustrating for you.

Take a moment to reflect on why those situations might be especially annoying for you personally. Our armor tends to get most triggered by what strikes a personal nerve or links to our specific combination of longings and sensitivities.

Threats Self-Assessment:
What threats are happening for you?

Threats to Livelihood

- ☐ You aren't paid what you should be.
- ☐ Your pay was reduced.
- ☐ Your promotion is stalled.
- ☐ There's a risk that you could lose your job altogether.
- ☐ Peers work in your territory, endangering your commissions.

Threats to Success

- ☐ You want to do well but goals are very hard to hit.
- ☐ Problems outside of your control are leading you to be less successful.
- ☐ You got a worse performance evaluation than you deserve.
- ☐ You feel there is little chance of doing well because of systemic factors.
- ☐ You feel thwarted by more strategic peers who "play the game" better than you do.
- ☐ There's a risk you could "lose" or be seen as not "winning" compared to others.

Threats to Stability

- ☐ You're new, and no one seems available to help you get oriented.
- ☐ The organization has no clear structures or processes; everything seems run haphazardly.
- ☐ Roles and expectations aren't clear so you don't know what impact you can have.
- ☐ The stakes are high and one mistake could be devastating.
- ☐ Your leader or your peers show behaviors that make the environment feel confusing and unstable for you.

Threats to Control

- ☐ Other people can intrude on your work plans and undermine your progress.
- ☐ Your schedule can change anytime as a result of others' decisions.
- ☐ Your boss is unpredictable and often changes course.
- ☐ Peers don't stay "in their lane," leaving you less control over your area.
- ☐ The organization is so matrixed that it is unclear what you can truly lead.
- ☐ You feel you can't be in control of your own fate at work.

Threats to Harmony

- ☐ There is tension or conflict on the team.
- ☐ There are overly emotional interactions that derail work.
- ☐ The culture is unnecessarily competitive, and peers are pitted against each other.
- ☐ The evaluation system encourages only individual performance, not team collaboration.

Threats to Autonomy

- ☐ You have controlling, pressuring, or micromanaging leaders or peers.
- ☐ Restrictive rules limit your freedom to work in the way that is optimal for you.
- ☐ You have to collaborate with others who steer the work in a way you don't agree with.
- ☐ You don't have enough autonomy at your level, and you feel blocked from moving ahead.

Threats to Reputation

☐ Your capabilities are misunderstood, and others see you as underperforming.
☐ You get blamed for mistakes.
☐ Your relevance to the team isn't acknowledged or appreciated.
☐ You work with high-stakes partners whose opinion of your value could change in an instant.

Threats to Fairness

☐ Your performance is judged against unclear or unfair expectations.
☐ You aren't paid what you deserve or others at the same level get more pay.
☐ Resources are distributed unfairly—e.g., others get more staff than you do.
☐ Work is distributed unfairly; you have to do more than others at the same level.
☐ Promotion speed or career growth has been slower than your peers.
☐ More praise is given to peers, while your success doesn't get the same notice.
☐ You work with others who don't play by the rules and who still get ahead.

Threats to Authority

☐ Your subordinates don't respect your role as a leader.
☐ Your reports get more respect from your boss than you do.
☐ People go around you for answers or help, undermining your authority or role.
☐ Your reports say "yes" to you in meetings but then make different decisions on their own.

Threats to Belonging

☐ You report with others to one boss, but there is no sense of being a part of a team.
☐ Your area is siloed and disconnected from the larger company's initiatives.
☐ You are left out of key meetings/projects.
☐ You are left out of social groups at work.
☐ There are cliques at work.

Threats to Dignity

☐ You are seen as more junior than you are.
☐ You are embarrassed publicly in a meeting.
☐ You are the focus of gossip.
☐ You are moved into a role of lower status.
☐ You, your voice, or your contribution to the work are ignored.

Other Threats

_____
_____
_____

Of the threats that are happening, which cause you the most frustration?

Owning My Armor Summary Worksheet

Here's what I tend to feel frustrated or threatened by on this team:

- [ ] _____
- [ ] _____
- [ ] _____
- [ ] _____
- [ ] _____
- [ ] _____
- [ ] _____
- [ ] _____
- [ ] _____
- [ ] _____
- [ ] _____
- [ ] _____

How do you react to what irks you?

Using the threats you identified on the Threats Self-Assessment, consider how you react to those threats. It may be helpful to ask yourself, what do I typically do in response to this frustrating situation or when dealing with an aggravating person?

For some of us, our typical reaction is "flight," and for others it's "fight." And sometimes we react to threats or frustrations with a combination of both: maybe we first react with flight, and then as the threat grows, we switch to fight, and even back to flight again if that isn't changing anything for us.

Another way to recognize your armor is to think about your Evil Twin: you on your worst day. What are you like on your worst day? How you act on your worst day is likely how your armor typically shows up: something aggravates you, and you react with your armor.

OWN
YOUR
ARMOR

Armor Self-Assessment Instructions

On the next page is a checklist of ways that people armor up to cope with threats. As you read through each kind of armor, check those you sometimes use at work. Note that the list of armor types isn't exhaustive. There are many variations and degrees of armored reactions. Use the list to prompt your own thinking about how best to describe your armor.

After a first pass through the list, review what you have checked and highlight which types of armor you tend to use the most. You might also go back to the threats you checked and ask yourself: What armor (aka coping mechanisms) do I use to deal with these threats?

Of course, we all have different degrees of armor at different times. Some mildly frustrating situations will bring out a mild reaction, while others bring out your fullest set of armor. Note some of those differences on your worksheet.

When you are under threat, what type of armor do you use?

FIGHT ARMOR:

- ☐ Advocate strongly for your position in debates
- ☐ Advocate strongly for more resources
- ☐ Take charge to get results
- ☐ Speak up in meetings, take more airtime
- ☐ Advise others how to do a better job
- ☐ Demand/command/yell
- ☐ Insist you are right
- ☐ Push for resolution now
- ☐ Take control, make rules
- ☐ Decisively create or change processes
- ☐ Complain/protest/lead pushback
- ☐ Tout your strengths and achievements
- ☐ Step up so you can stand out and prove yourself against unfair judgment
- ☐ Micromanage
- ☐ Push your way in, push others out
- ☐ Build alliances, build your strategic position
- ☐ Overwork, don't delegate
- ☐ Work around slower colleagues
- ☐ Work around ineffective leaders
- ☐ Point out problems you see
- ☐ Speak out against injustice
- ☐ Find allies to help fight poor leadership or key causes
- ☐ Be the comforter when others have complaints

FLIGHT ARMOR:

- ☐ Accommodate/appease to end the tension
- ☐ Avoid conflict
- ☐ Take control by being extra cautious
- ☐ Deflect feedback, blame others
- ☐ Explain how you are misunderstood
- ☐ Don't admit mistakes, deny responsibility
- ☐ Change the subject
- ☐ Intellectualize to avoid emotion
- ☐ Escalate to boss rather than deal with coworker
- ☐ Divest caring about outcomes
- ☐ Withdraw effort, initiate less
- ☐ Procrastinate on annoying tasks
- ☐ Be less collaborative, work head down
- ☐ Prevent criticism by asking for or waiting for guidance before starting in a wrong direction
- ☐ Preserve your autonomy by trying to avoid those who are intrusive or controlling
- ☐ Just do your job, focus on your own deliverables and not others' emergencies
- ☐ Rebel by doing less
- ☐ Keep silent when you see injustice
- ☐ Tune out emotional noise by staying professional, rational, objective
- ☐ Avoid coworkers when they are annoying.

Actually, some of those characters hit close to home.

I think my armor shows up in some ways like...

(See next page for refresher of the sample team armor)

- **The Chaos Clearer**
- **The Thwarted Achiever**
- **The Pressured New Guy**
- **The Feedback Frozen**
- **The Deep Focuser**
- **The Principled Warrior**
- **The Comforter**
- **The Drama Deflector**

Of all the armor you have used, which types do you think you use most?

_____

_____

_____

_____

Which do you use but wish you didn't?

_____

_____

_____

_____

Sample Team: Types of Armor

KEY VALUES AT STAKE	PERCEIVED THREATS
 **SUCCESS, CONTROL**	**IT SEEMS LIKE...** • Goals are challenging; progress toward them is too slow. • Processes aren't smooth; there's chaos in the system. • Others' less optimal efforts put your success at risk. Experienced as risk of failure and loss of control.
SUCCESS, REPUTATION	**IT SEEMS LIKE . . .** • Goals are challenging; progress toward them is too slow. • Others' less optimal efforts put your success at risk. • Obstacles around you make you look less productive. Experienced as a risk of failure, and risk of being misjudged.
 **REPUTATION, SUCCESS**	**IT SEEMS LIKE...** • Performance feedback hasn't been as positive as expected. • You feel your capabilities have been misunderstood. • There's pressure to perform and to appear successful quickly. Experienced as risk of being misjudged as failing or not meeting expectations.
 **REPUTATION CONTROL SUCCESS**	**IT SEEMS LIKE...** • Performance feedback has been negative and you feel misunderstood. • Pressure to quickly fix your reputation creates anxiety, which makes it harder to perform, yielding more criticism. Experienced as hopelessly trapped by endless criticism.
 **AUTONOMY, STABILITY, SUCCESS**	**IT SEEMS LIKE...** • Your boss or peers are controlling, pressuring, or micromanaging, which feels destabilizing and intrusive. • Engaging with them only slows you down, makes it harder to do your job, and leads to redoing work. Experienced as interference with your ability to control your own success.
 **FAIRNESS, LIVELIHOOD, SUCCESS**	**IT SEEMS LIKE...** • Compensation and promotion processes are unfair. • Protocols aren't followed, so work is distributed unequally, and some are more burdened than others. No one else speaks up about it. Experienced as unfair and limiting to livelihood and success.
 **HARMONY, BELONGING, SUCCESS**	**IT SEEMS LIKE...** • Instead of team cohesion, there is complaining, tension, and conflict, and some people aren't acting professionally. • Success seems impossible in such a negative environment. • Leader doesn't seem to make the changes necessary to improve things. Experienced as isolating, agitating, and interfering with productivity.
STABILITY, SUCCESS	**IT SEEMS LIKE...** • There is complaining, conflict, and emotional drama in the team, and some people aren't acting professionally. • Time is wasted, stability is threatened, and the work gets derailed by all the overemotional drama. Experienced as distracting and undermining of productivity.

COPING ACTIONS (ARMOR)

UNINTENDED IMPACT

SO UNDERSTANDABLY, YOU...

Push for results and take charge to accomplish the task.
Create/change processes quickly.
Direct, manage, or work around "thwarters."

BUT UNFORTUNATELY, YOUR ARMOR...

- Threatens others by coming across as controlling, critical, undervaluing of others, or micromanaging.

SO UNDERSTANDABLY, YOU...

Point out the problems you see so that they can be fixed.
Make it clear you are being misjudged by clarifying that your success is impeded by outside obstacles or other people, not your own abilities.

BUT UNFORTUNATELY, YOUR ARMOR...

- Threatens others by coming across as blaming, complaining, or not taking responsibility.

SO UNDERSTANDABLY, YOU...

Highlight achievements in meetings so your success gets noticed.
Downplay mistakes and push back against unfair negative feedback.
Make sure you get high-value work so you can stand out.

BUT UNFORTUNATELY, YOUR ARMOR...

- Threatens others by coming across as self-promoting, overly competitive, land-grabbing, rejecting of feedback, and not a team player.

SO UNDERSTANDABLY, YOU...

Try to take control of the situation by being extra cautious, taking it slowly to avoid making mistakes.
Prevent criticism by asking for or waiting for guidance before starting in a wrong direction.

BUT UNFORTUNATELY, YOUR ARMOR...

- Threatens others by coming across as slow moving, unproductive, unresponsive to feedback, and not taking initiative to contribute.

SO UNDERSTANDABLY, YOU...

- Preserve your autonomy by avoiding those who are intrusive or controlling.
- Just do your job and focus on your own deliverables.
- Don't automatically respond to people's "emergencies."

BUT UNFORTUNATELY, YOUR ARMOR...

- Threatens others by coming across as self-oriented, uncommunicative, and not willing to help others deliver what they need to deliver.

SO UNDERSTANDABLY, YOU...

- Advocate strongly for more pay, promotion, or resources.
- Find allies to speak out against injustice.
- If leaders aren't responsive, take it to their superiors.
- Highlight the obvious values that are being ignored.

BUT UNFORTUNATELY, YOUR ARMOR...

- Threatens others by coming across as combative, self-righteous, complaining, or challenging to leaders.

SO UNDERSTANDABLY, YOU...

- Try to create community by engaging with people
- Become a good listener, letting people vent their complaints about the leader or about each other.
- Help everyone feel heard and supported.

BUT UNFORTUNATELY, YOUR ARMOR...

- Threatens others by coming across as stirring the pot and encouraging a culture of gossip and complaining.
- Can be seen as wasting time on drama, undermining leaders, and not focusing enough on getting work done.

SO UNDERSTANDABLY, YOU...

- Tune out the emotional noise by staying professional and objective.
- Remind coworkers to focus on work, not pandering to people's "feelings."
- Defend your solutions as the rational ones.

BUT UNFORTUNATELY, YOUR ARMOR...

- Threatens others by coming across as indifferent to others' concerns/feelings, unwilling to listen, and dismissive of feedback that doesn't fit your definition of "rational."

Owning My Armor Summary Worksheet

 I tend to react with this armor:

☐ _____

☐ _____

☐ _____

☐ _____

☐ _____

☐ _____

☐ _____

☐ _____

☐ _____

☐ _____

☐ _____

☐ _____

Own Your Impact

It can be hard to admit, but when you are acting from your armored self, it isn't pretty.

How might your reactions to frustration look to those around you? If you are truly honest with yourself, what trouble can your armored reactions cause for others?

What threats might your armor create for others, and how might it impact team dynamics?

OWN
YOUR
IMPACT

Impact Self-Assessment Instructions

On the next page is a checklist of ways that people react to armor they see in others. As you read through each kind of impact, reflect on your own armored behavior and how it might impact other people you work with. This is the moment to try to put yourself completely into others' shoes. This is *not* the time to give yourself the benefit of the doubt or to assume, "People understand why I work the way I do" or "No one is really affected except those that need to be!"

Instead, let yourself wonder about what your armor looks like to others in the worst-case scenario. Even if your coping armor is totally justified, in what ways could it still annoy others or add to a tense culture?

There are many variations and degrees of reactions to armor and impact. Use the list to prompt your own thinking about how best to describe what others might be experiencing.

After a first pass through the list, review what you have checked and highlight which kind of impact might be the most likely reactions to your armor. Note them on the worksheet.

What is the impact of your armor?

FIGHT ARMOR:

When I am armored, it can cause others to feel...

- ☐ steered, overridden
- ☐ blocked and unheard
- ☐ demeaned, treated like children
- ☐ told they are wrong
- ☐ judged, criticized
- ☐ controlled, a loss of autonomy
- ☐ attacked, ganged up on
- ☐ micromanaged
- ☐ undervalued
- ☐ caught in unnecessary competition, like they have to fight for credit
- ☐ excluded
- ☐ defeated, played, drawn into politics, undermined
- ☐ that I'm self-promoting or self-oriented
- ☐ that I'm combative, or too challenging to the leader
- ☐ intruded upon, that I'm land-grabbing and in their lane
- ☐ that I'm self-righteous
- ☐ that I complain too much
- ☐ that I stir the pot or encourage gossip and complaining
- ☐ that I waste too much time on drama and not on work
- ☐ that I'm contributing to the erosion of trust

FLIGHT ARMOR:

When I am armored, it can cause others to feel...

- ☐ blamed
- ☐ that their feedback to me isn't heard
- ☐ exasperated that I don't listen well enough
- ☐ abandoned
- ☐ that their interests are minimized or sacrificed
- ☐ that I'm adding negativity or resentment to the culture
- ☐ that I don't take enough responsibility, or that others need to pick up my slack or carry more than their fair share
- ☐ that others have to initiate or nothing gets done
- ☐ unsuccessful because deadlines can get missed
- ☐ that I'm self-oriented
- ☐ that I'm uncollaborative or not a team player
- ☐ that I complain too much
- ☐ that I'm indifferent to others' concerns/feelings
- ☐ that I'm seeing them as irrational
- ☐ that I don't let conflict get resolved
- ☐ that direct communication is stopped or thwarted
- ☐ that I'm uncommunicative
- ☐ that I'm contributing to an erosion of trust

Be truly honest with yourself: how might your armor (your reaction to threats) impact other people you work with?

_____

_____

_____

_____

_____

_____

_____

_____

_____

_____

_____

_____

_____

_____

_____

_____

_____

_____

_____

_____

_____

_____

_____

Owning My Armor Summary Worksheet

 I realize my armor can have this impact on others:

☐ _____

☐ _____

☐ _____

☐ _____

☐ _____

☐ _____

☐ _____

☐ _____

☐ _____

☐ _____

☐ _____

☐ _____

...ng My Armor Summary Worksheet

Here's what I tend to feel frustrated or threatened by on this team:

☐ _____

☐ _____

☐ _____

I tend to react with this armor:

☐ _____

☐ _____

☐ _____

I realize my armor can have this impact on others:

☐ _____

☐ _____

☐ _____

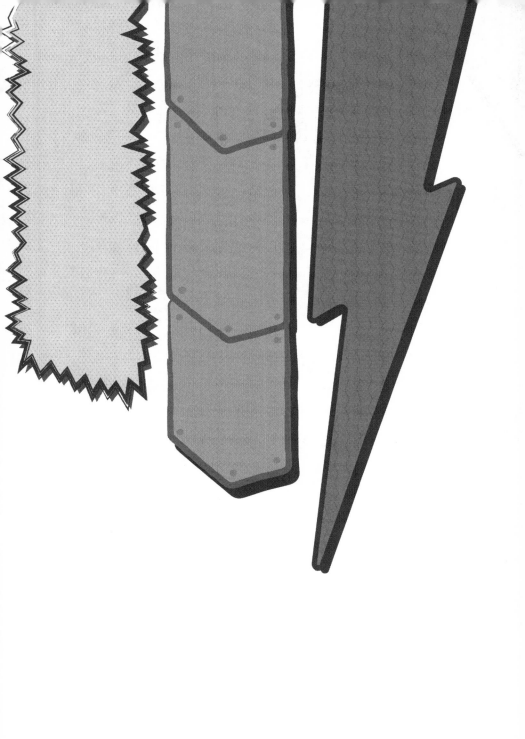

OWN YOUR ARMOR

PRINCIPLE #8

COMMUNICATION

Team Culture is Healed by Having Own-Your-Armor Conversations

From Own-Your-Armor Reflection to Own-Your-Armor Conversations

Since too much armor is what causes bad team dynamics, the key to changing culture is to remove armor and return to interacting with each other in an unarmored, Core way.

Own Your Armor Conversations are the key tools for removing armor.

Once you have done the work to understand and own your armor, you can have a productive conversation with another person about it. An Own Your Armor conversation is a way of declaring "I'm going to put down my armor because I know it is contributing to our problems," and inviting others to do so as well.

What does an Own Your Armor conversation look like?

Let's imagine an ideal Own Your Armor conversation between two members of the example team. Recall that Sandhya and Alvaro have slipped into a Charging-Dodging cycle because of the way their armor interacted.

To shift from that armored interaction to a more productive unarmored one, Sandhya and Alvaro would individually reflect on and answer the three key Own Your Armor questions for themselves:

- **Own your threats:** What threats make me put my armor on?
- **Own your armor:** What is my armor? What behavior and actions do I do to attempt to protect myself from threat?
- **Own your impact:** How might the armor I use contribute to threats the other person may experience?

Next, they would speak to each other about what they understand about their own threats, armor, and impact.

Here's how the conversation might go.

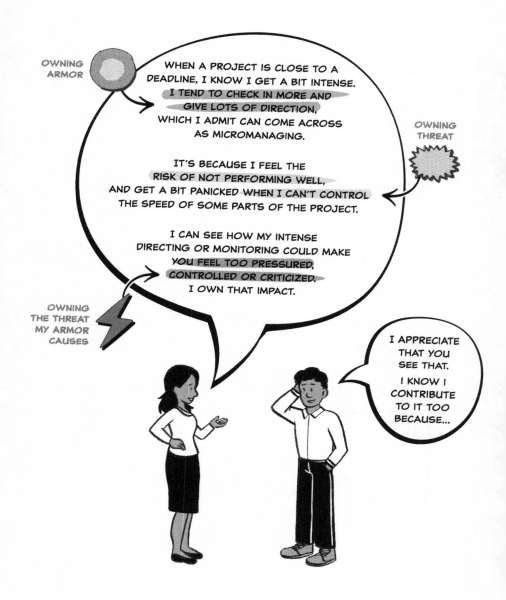

*Notice that Sandhya starts with owning her *armor*, then owns her *threats* and then her *impact*, while Alvaro starts with his *threat*, then his *armor*, and then its *impact*. The order in which you mention them isn't as important as mentioning

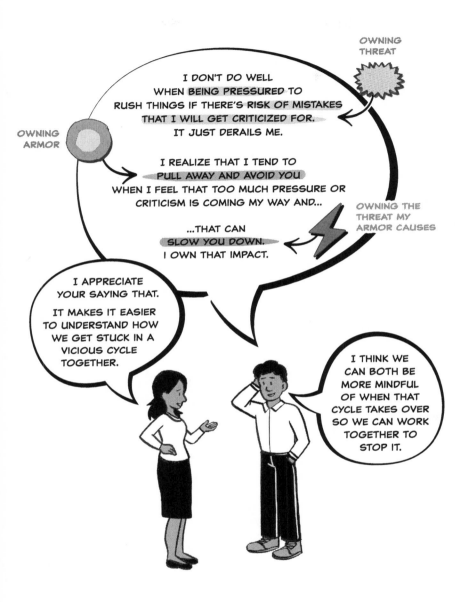

all of them and being clear that you are owning what *you* do that has negative impact on *others*. Talking about what *others* do that has impact on *you* is feedback; talking about what you do that has impact on others is owning.

"Okay, that sounds great," you might be thinking, "but no one in my workplace talks like that!

No one would ever admit they are doing something wrong!" And you would be right. Most of us have a pretty hard time vulnerably addressing someone who seems like an adversary this way and admitting how we contributed badly to the interaction.

But what if the other person owned their armor first? You might be a little suspicious, but if they genuinely owned their contribution to the tension, it might be quite disarming. Literally. If an adversary puts down their armor first, most of us would be much more likely to let down our own guard and respond more vulnerably. The only question is, who disarms first?

On teams, I wouldn't expect anyone to admit their armor is having a bad impact on others unless *everyone admits it*. It's like solving a Rubik's cube: all sides are involved and need simultaneous attention. So how can you get everyone to acknowledge their armor together?

Simultaneous armor owning usually happens at a specialized kind of offsite that offers the safety and setup to help everyone notice and own their armor together. The first step at such an event is to have everyone take some time to reflect on their own armor, knowing that the entire team has that same homework.

At the offsite, in a space of psychological safety, each person speaks about and takes individual ownership for their armor and its impact on others. As team members hear others owning their armor, there is a palpable sense of relief as the armor falls away and people show up more as their Core selves. That breaks the ice, but the work isn't over. The discussion then moves to how everyone's armor unintentionally intersects and to specific commitments to change armor-threat cycles.

Here's a glimpse of how the armor-owning part of such a discussion might go.

Notice that each person owns their armor *and* its impact.

In contrast, just mentioning what threatens you and how you respond ("I disengage because you are all too dramatic!") is unproductive justifying; it is not owning your armor.

You know you are in the right territory if when trying to own your armor *it makes you feel a little vulnerable.* Owning means you are acknowledging your behavior isn't perfect and that it is affecting others negatively. Saying so would make anyone feel a little exposed. But the spirit of an offsite like this is that we take that risk with each other, opening up what is real, because on the other side of that exposure is the possibility of understanding, appreciation, and trust.

If a full-team dialogue like this feels overwhelming, start one on one. Who in the team might you have negatively impacted with your armor? Invite them to do the self-reflection on threats, armor, and impact, and then invite them to dialogue with you.

Most teams need an external coach or HR professional to help run a session like this, primarily because the leader is also involved in the team dynamic. That means they can't just facilitate the session; they need to fully participate and complete the same Own Your Armor preparation as the rest of the team.

Own Your Armor conversations can feel like hard work.

You might be wondering: how bad off does a team need to be to invest in this kind of work? I'd say the trust building that comes from having Own Your Armor conversations actually is best to do before the dynamics are too locked up. If trust is eroding, collaboration is slipping, or bad behaviors are increasing, that is the moment to pause and initiate these conversations. Even when teams are operating fairly well, having the language to talk about threat and potential armor can help a team handle the moments of reactivity to threats that will inevitably come in the future.

In fact, as soon as you sense that there is "bad communication" on your team, it is a sign of armoring. When people feel too uncomfortable or threatened to speak openly and directly with each other, they begin to speak and act in armored ways—indirectly, passive-aggressively, not saying what they really mean, and getting what they need in self-oriented ways. Trying to solve communication problems when everyone is in their guarded, armored, Evil Twin state usually only makes the vicious communication cycles persist.

Good communication is unarmored. The purpose of all Own Your Armor conversations is to return everyone to their Core selves, by taking the vulnerable step of sharing your understanding of how your armor works.

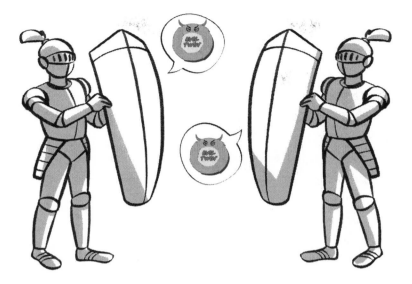

"Bad communication" is armored

"Good communication" is unarmored

Differences in Armor Stuckness

Even if everyone has the same homework for owning their armor, different people can be at very different places in their understanding of the motives and patterns of their behavior. Some people have a deep understanding of themselves, while others don't have as much insight into what triggers their own reactions. Some people are more open to examining their impact, and others are more tightly armored and less open.

Team members or leaders who are more aware or less armored can lead the way in helping others in the team own their armor. When more open team members let their guard down and talk openly about imperfect reactions, it can serve as an invitation for others to introspect as well.

And finally, team dynamics sometimes do take a few "repair loops" for the armor to come fully off. A one-time intervention or conversation just starts the process of turning a vicious cycle into a virtuous one, but true change needs reinforcement and revisiting. An Own Your Armor conversation—whether as a full team or one on one—may take more than one try, but it gets easier with each conversation. Imagine that in the first conversation you just agree on one thing: "We all have had some negative impact on one another with our armor." When you say that, you are acknowledging that both (or all) sides have contributed and that your armor is not your best self—there is a much better you (and them) available once you sort this out. That simple admission can cause relief, as you begin to see each other as the kind of people who are *willing* to talk about their contribution to the tension. That already makes your colleague(s) seem more reasonable. The next conversation is then less risky, and you'll all be more likely to more specifically admit what your contribution of armor and impact has been.

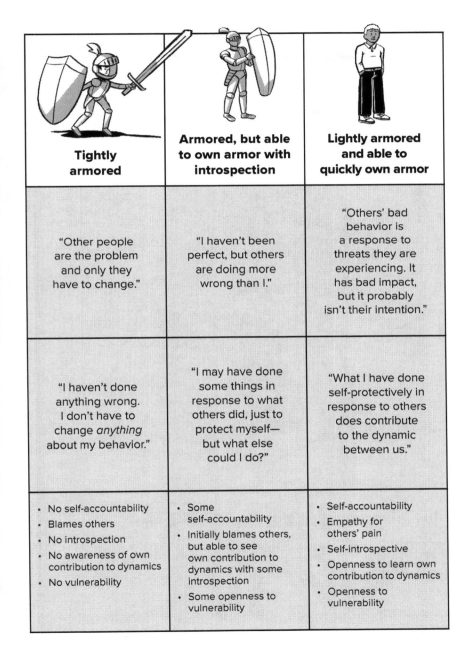

Tightly armored	Armored, but able to own armor with introspection	Lightly armored and able to quickly own armor
"Other people are the problem and only they have to change."	"I haven't been perfect, but others are doing more wrong than I."	"Others' bad behavior is a response to threats they are experiencing. It has bad impact, but it probably isn't their intention."
"I haven't done anything wrong. I don't have to change *anything* about my behavior."	"I may have done some things in response to what others did, just to protect myself— but what else could I do?"	"What I have done self-protectively in response to others does contribute to the dynamic between us."
• No self-accountability • Blames others • No introspection • No awareness of own contribution to dynamics • No vulnerability	• Some self-accountability • Initially blames others, but able to see own contribution to dynamics with some introspection • Some openness to vulnerability	• Self-accountability • Empathy for others' pain • Self-introspective • Openness to learn own contribution to dynamics • Openness to vulnerability

What If Someone Just Won't Own Their Armor?

Even so, no matter what you do, some people may still resist acknowledging that they have armor or never let their guard down. What can be done about them?

There is an old Aesop's fable that describes a power battle between the Wind and the Sun. The Wind boasts, "It is obvious that I am the more powerful force in the world! See how everything down on Earth yields to my gales." The Sun counters, "Are you so sure? How about we duel it out

to see who is more powerful?" With delight, the Wind agrees and points out a man walking along below them. "See that man? Watch how easily I will blow his coat and hat off!" The Wind gathers all its strength and blows, buffeting the man with swirls of pressure. The more the Wind blows, the more the man bends over, puts his back to the wind, and tightly holds onto his coat and hat. The Sun says, "Step aside, Wind, and I will show you how it is done!" The Sun shines brightly, and within minutes, the man takes off his hat and coat.

Armor Doesn't Yield to Pressure

Armor is like our coat and hat. We almost never take off armor under pressure from others, or when we get signals that the environment isn't safe enough.

Common efforts to help another person take off their armor often come across as an ominous wind:

- "You are being very defensive."
- "Do something about your anger management issues."
- "I have some feedback about your problematic people skills."
- "Your behavior is causing harm to others."

Telling someone that they are being defensive almost never will make them be less defensive. Instead, it reads as judgment and mistrust—more threat—which makes people feel the need to armor up even more.

Remove the Threat to Remove Armor

How, then, to create the "sunshine" that will entice someone to take off their own armor? In an environment of psychological safety, freedom from threat and empathy, armor isn't needed, and we naturally take it off.

Most of us get less defensive when:

- Someone is showing genuine care for our troubles.

- We feel heard; our complaints or pain are not dismissed.

- We are seen as a good person generally, and our armor is seen as self-protective in a tough situation (e.g., "There must be a good reason why you are armored.").

- Someone acknowledges what we are up against (e.g., "The pandemic has made it particularly tough for parents of young kids, so I know it's so hard to be at your usual best.").

- Someone else owns their side of a conflict first (e.g., "We've had some friction and I know I contributed by...").

The best way to help someone else own their armor is to lead by owning yours, and to recognize that some of your armor might actually be creating threat for the other person. "I notice you haven't been eager to collaborate lately. Is there something I am doing that is making you withdraw?"

For colleagues who are tightly armored, it's very tempting to think of them as deficient in emotional intelligence or skills. Try instead to consider that they may have a very strong need for self-protection and legitimate reasons for keeping their armor on longer than others. Empathy for why their armor is thick will go a long way toward helping them join the team in owning it.

"He is behaving badly because he is a bad worker, has a bad personality, or is missing essential people skills."

"He is behaving badly because he is armored. Something must be threatening him."

For those more tightly armored, sometimes just learning the Own Your Armor principles begins to open their mindset and allows them to see their own challenges differently. Understanding that armoring is universal, and how threats and armor operate in others, can begin to spark introspection about how those processes work for oneself. Just recognizing that their armored self isn't as productive as who they are at the Core is a milestone in itself, which can encourage motivation for getting back to their Core.

Other Applications for an Own Your Armor Conversation

In addition to helping a team get to the bottom of its dysfunctional dynamics, Own Your Armor conversations are also useful for many common workplace challenges. The Own Your Armor approach begins with a key mindset change: that bad behavior, conflict, and disagreement are not caused by bad people, but by a pileup of armor. Here are three examples of how that mindset can change the outcome of complicated communication challenges.

- **Leader-report feedback** When leaders find that their report just isn't accepting feedback, it's an opportunity to consider if there could be an armored cycle happening between the report and the manager. Is the employee armoring up in response to your micromanager armor? Are they shutting down because they are frozen with feedback? Learning about your report's perceived threats and resulting armor gives you a chance to empathize and help them return to their Core (see example pages 96 and 97).

- **Leaders mediating peer-to-peer conflict** When team members are in conflict, their leader can serve as an unbiased mediator if the leader sees that the "bad behavior" on both sides is actually armored behavior. Both sides can be encouraged to own their armor as a way to resolve the conflict.

- **Cross-functional teams in conflict** Instead of viewing the other team as "the problem," notice the ways that the teams are unintentionally threatening one another's success. If both teams feel thwarted by the other's actions, both will armor up, causing more viciously circular obstacles to collaboration. Resolution can happen when both teams own the armor that they have been using that has negatively impacted the other team.

DEFENSIVE AGAINST FEEDBACK

MEDIATING CONFLICT

CROSS-FUNCTIONAL CHALLENGES

OWN YOUR ARMOR

PRINCIPLE #9

LEADER ARMOR

Leader Armor Has an Outsized Impact on the Team

What about the leader?

When introducing the example team, I didn't specify which of the eight people is the leader. Intentionally. Because leader armor can take any of these forms.

Leaders respond to threats that include external market threats, pressure from their own leaders, pressure to produce, and pressure to be a good team leader. And they respond to these threats with armor, just like anyone else. The difference is that their armor has an even bigger impact on team members and the team culture.

If the leader of this team is Alain, he might be beloved as a person for his efforts to bring harmony to the team, but he might also cause frustration if he has less focus on directing progress on goals. A team might be driven and productive under a leader like Sandhya, but also exhausted and cautious about initiating any ideas that might be different from her plans. Tor as a leader might try to never contend with the "drama" and instead keep it all Under the Table, where it still affects everyone but is now impossible to address. You can imagine every one of these characters as the leader and predict the impact of that style of armor on the team.

Leader armor matters and needs to be owned. But it takes a courageous leader to vulnerably own their armor.

What doesn't work: Leaders who try to effect change by seeing the team as the problem

When team dynamics are tense, if the leader tells others to own their contributions but isn't comfortable doing so themselves, the team will resist as well—it's just too risky. When leaders don't own their armor, the team usually settles into a stance of blaming the leader for the dysfunction, because it's a comfortable self-protective place for the team members to sit ("It's not my problem, it's the leader's—and I'm not seeing any great leadership!"). That whispered or not-whispered criticism then becomes another threat to the leader. If he or she doubles down with more armor and no owning, the dynamic grows, and it gets exceedingly more difficult for the leader to lead.

Imagine a culture offsite called by such a leader. Everyone on the team might know the leader's armor is a key ingredient, but it's too risky to say it out loud. If the leader isn't owning their armor, certainly no one else will. Perhaps the team will go through the charade of discussing what should change to improve the culture without actually addressing the real cause—the clashing armor, including that of the leader.

What does work: The leader goes first...

A team leader's armor owning also tends to have an outsized contribution in a positive direction. A team leader who vulnerably owns their armor will lead the way for the rest of the team to do so as well. Imagine a leader of a team in tension taking the time to own their impact, threats, or armor by saying things like:

- "I know I'm pushing you guys very hard, and I realize now that it's adding stress" **(owning impact).**

- "I have to admit I'm worried about our perfor-mance against the quarterly goals **(owning threats)** and that is probably causing me to be more micromanaging" **(owning armor)**.

- "I'm noticing the team is taking less initia-tive than you all used to. Is there something I'm doing that is causing it? What might I be missing?" **(owning and inquiring about impact).**

Team members appreciate hearing what the leader is up against, and if it is shared in a spirit of vulnerability and openness to partnership, it can open the door to powerfully different conversations.

OWN YOUR
ARMOR

PRINCIPLE #10

TEAM STRENGTH

**Owning Your Armor Unlocks
Team Strengths and Restores
Healthy Culture**

A team that takes an Own Your Armor approach to its Under-the-Table dynamics has a tremendous amount to gain.

Owning your armor deepens trust, improves team relationships, and changes culture, but it also unlocks individual strengths and a team's best performance.

Individual Strengths Are Hidden by Armor

Recall that every one of us has two states of operating. When we aren't under threat, we operate from our Core state, and we show the best of our strengths, thinking, and interpersonal skills.

But under threat, we armor up, and those strengths and skills are not as visible. We come across as our "Evil Twin" and a lot less appealing to our teammates.

As a result, a team under threat—an armored team—will be much less productive than an unarmored one. The team's strengths are suffocated as everyone focuses on surviving threats.

If only we could vacuum up threats, teams would be so much more high-performing ...

Threat in the Environment

When the environment is **low threat**—supportive, with clear expectations and roles—success is possible and we feel respected, fairly evaluated, and connected with others. As a result, we can stay in our Core selves, do what needs to be done, and interact smoothly with the team. Armor mostly stays in the closet. When inevitable threats come (because it's impossible to avoid threats in any work environment), people will armor up. But if a team takes the time to understand threats, and each person recognizes their own armor and the impact it can have, teams can move rather quickly back to Core, and back to high levels of trust and productivity.

In contrast, when the environment is **high threat**—where external or internal threats are uncontrolled, minimized, or undiscussed—armor will go on and stay on. If the armor isn't owned, interpersonal threats will mount, and more armor will pile on. Teams can certainly operate and get work done when armored, but the culture will noticeably sag, trust will drain away, team members' motivation will dip, and when the emotional cost gets too high, people will leave.

Acknowledging threats and owning armor begins to break the cycle, and gives the team an opportunity to return to health.

Unlocking Individual Strengths

Remember, owning armor doesn't require changing anyone's personality. Instead, when team members return to operating from their Core selves, everyone's strengths are fully unlocked for the benefit of the enterprise.

When everyone is unarmored, the team appreciates Sandhya's organizational skills, and Grace and Carl's drive for results. Alvaro's conservative tendencies, Tor's professionalism, and Kaila's high sense of responsibility keep the team from making big mistakes. Justine's focus on fairness and Alain's empathy productively maintain a sense of community. Team members appreciate the diversity of what others bring to the group and rely on each other's counterbalanced powers.

Unlocking Team Strengths

Everyone wants to work on a team that is high performing and collaborative, and where communication is easy and productive. We want uncomplicated dynamics with our colleagues so we can use our talents to have the most impact and feel valued and respected. When you look Under the Table at such a dream team, there's lots of psychological safety and few threats, so there's little need to armor up and everyone can stay in their best selves. Teamwork is strong and everyone feels supported to excel.

When threats present themselves, like challenging market conditions or conflict between colleagues, team members might armor up. But a team whose members can reflect on their threat response and own their armor will be able to swiftly return to their Core selves and get on with their work. The more we understand our own and others' armor, the better able we will be to transform difficult cultures into teams we feel proud to be a part of.

SUMMARY

THE OWN YOUR ARMOR PRINCIPLES

PRINCIPLE #1: TABLE

Under-the-Table Dynamics Can't Be Solved with Above-the-Table Strategies *p. 18*

PRINCIPLE #2: THREATS

Threats and Armor Drive Bad Team Dynamics *p. 26*

PRINCIPLE #3: ARMOR

"Bad Apples" Are Usually Just Good People Trying to Protect Themselves *p. 38*

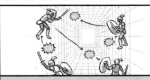

PRINCIPLE #4: EVERYONE

Everyone On the Team Contributes to the Dynamics *p. 70*

PRINCIPLE #5: CYCLE

Armor is Both a Response to Threat and a Cause of Threat, Causing Cycles *p. 98*

PRINCIPLE #6: INDIVIDUAL OWNING

To Change Dynamics, Armor Needs to Be Individually Owned *p. 108*

PRINCIPLE #7: THREE PARTS OF OWNING

Own Your Threats, Own Your Armor, Own Your Impact *p. 114*

PRINCIPLE #8: COMMUNICATION

"Good Communication" Is Unarmored *p. 150*

PRINCIPLE #9: LEADER ARMOR

Leader Armor has an Outsized Impact on the Team *p. 178*

PRINCIPLE #10: TEAM STRENGTH

Owning Armor Unlocks Team Strengths *p. 186*

Takeaways

Armoring:

- We all armor up when we feel we need to.

- Your armor is not your personality or your "true colors." It is your protective way of responding to threats.

- Armoring is normal. Armoring is a feature of being human, not a trait of "some defensive people."

- When in our armored state we are more likely to irritate or hurt others. Not because we intend to or want to. It's just that armor is cold and human relationships prefer warmth.

- When everyone around us is armoring up, we naturally follow suit. "People here don't care about each other; this is too risky a place for warmth or vulnerability," so with our armor, we add even more coldness to the environment. It happens at work and everywhere else in life.

- Armor creates uncomfortable culture, erodes trust in relationships, and sinks motivation and productivity.

Owning Armor:

- Your armor isn't your personality or your real self. When you own that you've armored up, you show that your armor and your real self are separate. The cold facade of self-protection falls away and reveals who you really are.

- Owning your armor includes owning your impact on others.

- Owning your armor isn't "apologizing"; it's an acknowledgment that you have armored up and that has had a negative impact on others.

- Owning armor repairs relationships because it brings understanding. Others understand you more ("Oh, that's why he seemed so different," or "Oh, that was what she was up against.") and others feel understood by you ("It's good to hear she gets what her impact is on others," or "What a relief that he gets how we all feel when he armors up.")

What's Next: Using the *Own Your Armor* Approach for Your Team

If I'm a leader who wants to run an *Own Your Armor* offsite, how do I do that?

Some leaders are naturally adept at vulnerably owning their own armor, and if you are one of those leaders, you can successfully lead your team in an Own Your Armor exercise. However, most leaders would be better off engaging a coach or HR professional to facilitate these events, which will help you as a leader participate as fully as everyone else. Find a coach who has trained in this method at OwnYourArmor.com.

We aren't quite ready to do an offsite. How can I get my team prepared for using the *Own Your Armor* approach for culture change?

Invite the members of your team to read the book and consider doing a team version of the Threat Assessment, where the team can talk openly about the threats that impact everyone. It is very powerful when a leader takes the time to understand the threats facing the team, whether they are market threats, cross-functional threats, performance threats for the entire team, individual interpersonal threats, or threats a leader may inadvertently be causing. Simply naming threats and planning to work on them together reduces the sense of individual threat and reduces armoring. Once you understand the threats your team faces, acknowledge them, and talk about them, you can begin to battle them as a team.

I'm a team member and want to have my team learn this approach, but I'm not sure our leader is on board. How should I handle that?

Invite your leader to read this book so they understand the mindset shift it represents and meet to discuss insights you both had. Tell other team members to check it out as well. If your leader appreciates the approach, offer to support the idea when they first pitch it to the team.

I'm a team member and want to start helping my team to Own our Armor. What can I start doing now?

Start with owning your own armor. Connect with a trusted colleague to practice an Own Your Armor conversation. Begin by completing the Threat, Armor, and Impact Self-assessments and then discuss how your armor might impact your colleague's. Notice what you learn from the exercise and consider sharing your experience with other team members.

I'm a coach or HR professional. How do I train to facilitate this kind of offsite?

Check out the training opportunities at our website: www.OwnYourArmor.com

How do I order multiple copies of *Own Your Armor* for my organization, association, conference, or clients who are business owners and leaders?

Learn about bulk discounts and place an order at: Info@OwnYourArmor.com.

I'd like to offer a keynote for my company, a training workshop for my HR/Learning teams, or a guided book club experience with the author.

Reach out to Dr. Brody:

LinkedIn.com/in/Dr-Michelle-Brody
www.MichelleBrody.com.

Acknowledgments

There was a lot of serendipity that led to the creation of this book, and I'm so grateful for it. Somehow, the right people came into my life at just the right time to guide me along at each important phase.

Four years after I published my first book, *Stop the Fight!*, I thought I was retiring as a writer and I went back to doing my two day jobs—as an executive coach to leaders and teams, and as a psychologist for couples.

But just before the pandemic, two wonderful writers gave me the push I needed to start writing again. Thank you, Joanna Faber and Julie King, authors of *How to Talk When Kids Won't Listen*. You reached out to be introduced to the incredible Emily Tomasik Wimberly (who had illustrated *Stop the Fight!*), but our connection in 2019 set my intention to create what became *Own Your Armor*. Joanna and Julie, as we are all engaged in efforts to create peace in relationships, I benefitted tremendously from your encouragement, your on-point feedback, and your inspiring engagement in my progress.

2020 and 2021 brought much more time with my adult kids, so they were around to weigh in (and help sketch!) the early drawings of the sample team members and offer some daily feedback on early ideas. Eva, Jesse, and Lev, your input was so helpful and it was so much fun to have you around to brainstorm with me.

A chain of artist connections introduced me to the outstanding illustrator of this book, Lisa Naffziger. With your amazing ability for drawing teams in corporate settings, people would never guess that you're really a sci-fi graphic novelist (Yes! Look her up …). Lisa, I so appreciate your artistry, attention to detail, supreme patience, and just incredibly perfect capture of ideas in pictures. You are a truly talented artist and the most trusted partner to have alongside me in the creative trenches. Your art will always be the heart of *Own Your Armor*.

In two years of Zoom meetings, I met the most amazing new people in randomly assigned breakout rooms. That was how I met Dorothy Cantor, who I had admired when I was a young graduate student and she was the

president of the American Psychological Association. Dorothy, I cannot thank you enough for your generous mentorship on every imaginable aspect of the writing of this book. I couldn't have done it without you!

Sharmin Banu was another new breakout-room friend, and I will always be grateful to her for her introduction to Amanda Rooker of SplitSeed Media, the extraordinary editor who made every sentence of *Own Your Armor* better. Amanda, I was repeatedly amazed at how you managed to get to know this book so totally that you could so flexibly offer the most perfect suggestions for optimally organizing it. Your support was so genuine and your brilliance so clear.

Thanks also to Amanda for introducing me to the spectacular George Stevens, owner of G Sharp Design, LLC and the graphic designer whose genius resulted in the *Own Your Armor* cover and interior page design. George, your creativity is a boundless and otherworldly gift. I so appreciated your endless ideas, flexibility, and openness to keep searching to find the best solutions, all while being the most positive human one could be. You are such a pleasure to work with and what you designed is just exceptional.

The chain of fortuitous introductions continued when George connected me with another superstar—Kate Colbert of Silver Tree Communications—who had me asking myself again, "How did I get this lucky to work with such amazing people?" I'm convinced that Kate is the world's greatest publishing coach and book marketer. Kate, every minute of your counsel was of value. What a blessing it was to have you with your tremendous expertise at my side to ferry *Own Your Armor* through the publishing process and beyond.

I'm so grateful to the friends and family who offered to read through early drafts and kick the tires on my first ideas of what this book would be. Thank you to Suzie Marder, Diane Werner, Rachel Brody, Barbara Weiner, Mathew Lazarus, Martin Juhn, and Kate Berardo for those conversations and challenges that refined the direction. Thanks to the friends, clients, and colleagues who read the later drafts and offered the valuable feedback that took this book across the finish line: Karen Erikson, Todd Stern, Martin Juhn (again!), Ted Miller, Mara Lassner, and Lois Lustig. It meant the world to me that you all took the time to give my drafts such thoughtful and complete reads, and to be honest with me about how to improve the book.

Thank you to the many clients who trusted me to help them work through their team challenges, giving me the opportunity to learn and continue to refine the *Own Your Armor* approach. I was continuously energized to discover that the writing of this book was even more relevant than I initially hoped—that very experienced HR and L&D professionals appreciated how *Own Your Armor* principles helped their practice. There's nothing quite like that kind of validation. I'd like to especially thank the executives of the ERP networking group who invited me to try out much of the newest material in their meetings. Thank you to my coach colleagues, especially those at the Exetor Group, for all I have learned from working together with you.

To my wonderful parents, Marsha and Peter Brody. I have always felt your belief in me and your constant encouragement for all my endeavors. Your dedication as parents and your dedication to your work have been inspiring. Thank you to my sisters, my extended family, and community of friends for all your accompaniment, support, and interest as this book came together.

Eva, I so appreciate that as you are now old enough to experience workplace culture, you've shared powerful insights to make this book better. And what a treat that you have been a booster for me to speak at your workplace!

Jesse, you've made some critical saves with your feedback about the visual elements of this book! I have so appreciated that I could rely on you to offer a creative and difference-making opinion when it counts.

Lev, I'm so glad you were still here all the way through the writing of this book. You were there when the title popped into my head and were encouraging then and many times after. And it was always nice to end a late-night writing session and find you cooking your second dinner. . . .

Last and most, I want to thank Hal. You have encouraged me in every way, always listening, supporting, and believing in me. You read so many drafts, helped advise on tons of illustrations, and just were so in the process with me every step of the way. Thank you for making everything in my life more wonderful because you are in it.

About the Author

Michelle Brody, PhD, is an executive coach and a clinical psychologist who brings 25 years of experience in both corporate and family settings to the challenging problem of interactional conflict. Her specialty as a coach is in guiding teams that have complicated dynamics, and helping them reach greater collaboration, improve communication, and resolve tension.

Dr. Brody has coached and designed executive training programs across a wide range of industries, including technology, manufacturing, management consulting, marketing, academia, insurance, non-profit management, politics, healthcare, accounting, and law. She has worked with teams at global companies like Meta (Facebook), Siemens, and Alcoa, as well as for smaller companies, startups, and partnerships. She has been an invited speaker for corporate and community groups on topics related to team communication, team dynamics, and team collaboration. Dr. Brody has also served as a master trainer of psychologists, professional coaches, and HR and learning professionals.

Learn more and keep in touch with Dr. Brody at:

LinkedIn.com/in/Dr-Michelle-Brody
www.MichelleBrody.com.

Also by Michelle Brody, PhD:

Made in the USA
Columbia, SC
04 October 2024